WOMEN IN THE GOSPELS

Carlo M. Martini

WOMEN IN
THE GOSPELS

CROSSROAD • NEW YORK

1990

The Crossroad Publishing Company
370 Lexington Avenue, New York, NY 10017

Original title: *La donna nel suo popolo*
Copyright © 1987, Editrice Ancora, Milano, Italy
English translation copyright © St. Paul Publications,
England 1989

Printed in the United States of America

Library of Congress Cataloging-in-Publication Data

Martini, Carlo M.
[Donna nel suo popolo. English]
Women in the gospels/Carlo-Maria Martini.
p.   cm.
Translation of: La donna nel suo popolo.
ISBN 0-8245-0986-2
1. Women in the Bible—Meditations.   2. Bible. N.T. Gospels-
-Meditations.   I. Title.
BS2555.4.M328   1990
226'.0922'082—dc20
89-38788
CIP

CONTENTS

FOREWORD

This book contains retreat meditations that Cardinal Martini gave for 240 religious Sisters of his Archdiocese of Milan. In compliance with the wish of the 11,000 Sisters of the archdiocese, all were afforded the possibility of listening to the talks by radio and thus taking part in the retreat.

The Cardinal's words were extraordinarily rich and profound. As always, however, the written word does not convey the resonances of the voice, its intonation, emphasis, emotion, and the immediate warmth of oral communication. This seems worth mentioning to the reader.

It would be good to read this book in a context of prayer, because in keeping with the character of a retreat, the director merely proposes a "task", a personal, spiritual activity of reflection and openness to contemplation.

The title of this book could give a mistaken impression, as though it were simply a book about woman. In a certain sense it is, but not in the direction of the flood of books written during the past few decades on the problem of woman in today's world. "The *Planet Woman*," says Cardinal Martini (and we add: the "Planet Man" also), "is mysterious and cannot be easily fathomed." Only God who said, "'Let us make man in our image, after our likeness...' male and female he created them," can expound the mysterious depths of his creature. But God has spoken in the Bible.

In these meditations the Cardinal does nothing but look through the lens of gospel passages at some women portrayed there and then observe them in Mary's light or in contrast to her, an undertaking which is not as simple as it might seem. Mary – "she whose femininity is a sign of the supremely Other" because it is "the beginning of a new humanity in which God becomes flesh." Mary – who at the foot of the cross, where her motherhood assumes universal dimensions, repeats her yes of the Annunciation. Mary – who illuminates the whole of human history.

The author claims that he will limit himself to offering points for meditation and clues for personal reflection; that he will communicate the intuitions that the gospel passages arouse in him concerning the feminine reality. Without realizing it, he ends up by saying things about woman that perhaps have never yet been said. He does so by listening to God who speaks in Scripture.

We would like to add that this book is beneficial for every Christian, whether man or woman, in the search for the God of revelation, for it serves as a brief, simple and profound compendium of Catholic existential theology.

The "map" at the beginning of the book graphically represents the retreat itinerary. Transposing it into words, we can express it as follows: it is the concrete path that a person takes, by way of the gospel, towards total conformation to Christ in the Holy Spirit for the glory of God the Father. It is a way lit up by the person and life of Mary.

It is not easy in a few brush-strokes of contemplative reflection to picture the interior life together with its day-to-day practice in the life of the Christian. For this purpose, theology employs various disciplines that have to be harmonized and interpreted in order to avoid dangerous clefts between faith and life. Frequently the problem of a believer is that of passing from baptismal faith to adult faith, of successfully impregnating family, social, civil and political life with faith.

In an original and impressive way, Cardinal Martini brings faith down to the level of concrete daily life, directing all of the reality we experience to the sole Reality from whom everything proceeds and to whom it all returns.

MAP OF OUR SPIRITUAL JOURNEY

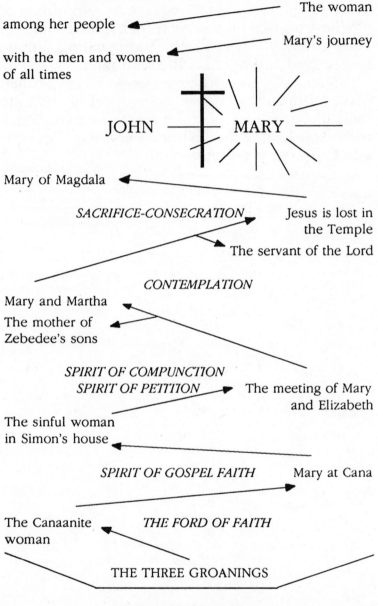

The woman

among her people

Mary's journey

with the men and women
of all times

JOHN ——+—— MARY ——

Mary of Magdala

SACRIFICE-CONSECRATION

Jesus is lost in
the Temple

The servant of the Lord

CONTEMPLATION

Mary and Martha

The mother of
Zebedee's sons

SPIRIT OF COMPUNCTION
SPIRIT OF PETITION

The meeting of Mary
and Elizabeth

The sinful woman
in Simon's house

SPIRIT OF GOSPEL FAITH   Mary at Cana

The Canaanite   *THE FORD OF FAITH*
woman

THE THREE GROANINGS

see page 109 for explanation

INTRODUCTION

This is the first time I am preaching to such a large group of religious who, moreover, do not all belong to the same community but represent all the Congregations of women present in the diocese. In you I see the person and vocation of woman in today's society: a multitude of millions of people of very diverse religious, human and social attitudes.

In prayer you bring before God the whole of humanity, typified and realized in Mary the woman. She is, in fact, the beginning of a new humanity in which God becomes flesh.

A message

I admit that I feel trepidation at my great responsibility and yet I have agreed to this undertaking for a very definite reason. It springs from my conviction that the crisis regarding the role of woman in society is the crossroads of many other social, human and religious problems of our times. So I have decided to send a message: *Let us save society!* This is a message that we shall understand better little by little as it emerges from the following meditations, which concern you, your mode of being and your choice of vocation in the full sense of the term, as a sign of a way of life and a search in faith that is valid for the whole of society. If I direct this message to you, it is because I feel that consecrated women are a precious pledge for saving the mission of woman in the world.

This is, then, a providential occasion for religious. It should help you to feel and to live your role genuinely and to assume serious responsiblity, above all for the women of our day. Obviously we are not concerned with acquiring a certain kind of knowledge or specializing in some branch, or with becoming inflated like the frog in the fable so we can rise to some position or other. Instead we intend to grasp the profound delicacy of your vocation as women and as consecrated persons, because it is precisely in this vocation that you are a sign of the righting of the actual role of woman in society. This is a difficult point to comprehend. All too often we expect the solution to various problems to come from some new heavenly army or by invoking some mysterious techniques. In reality it is already given to us, and the experience of this gift is the salvation manifested in an authentic existence, authentically expressed as such. Only in this way can your vocation enlighten others and make them recognize what is essential.

So there is a great deal at stake, namely, the response to a call. But even to become aware of our poverty and weakness, of our escapism when confronted with the call, is a way of being authentic. I would not want you to regard my words as mere concepts or information to be received, learned and then passed on verbatim. This is not my intention, for I realize that I am not capable of exploring alone what has been called the "Planet Woman". I shall give some pointers and suggestions; I shall communicate some of my intuitions, and you ought to dwell on the word of God in prayer and contemplation in order to enter into that mysterious planet and become explorers and guides on it.

The first great explorer and guide in the mystery of femininity is of course Mary. She teaches us that what counts is to be and to live and not just to say and to parrot words. This, then, is your fundamental mission: to be yourselves and thus to underline the importance of being over doing and of the word of God over words.

Our title

I propose to contemplate one sole gospel scene: *Mary at the foot of the cross.* Keeping this picture in mind, we shall meditate on a series of gospel scenes that permit us to make some reflections in the light or backlight of this one great scene.

Our title will be: "The woman among her people." The woman is first of all Mary as symbol of every woman who wishes to attain full self-realization, not alone but among her people. We can add a sub-title: "Mary's journey with the men and women of all times." Thus we shall contemplate Mary, desiring to see how she has gone her way and how we want to go ours with her.

On August 15, the solemnity of the Assumption, I went to visit the prisoners at St Victor's Jail in Milan. The programme did not include a visit to the women's section. So one of the Sisters brought me a booklet which the women prisoners had prepared for me, containing excerpts from letters, and some drawings and photographs. It began with the following sentence:

> There are days, anniversaries and feasts which, lived behind walls, far from one's dear ones and children, become sadder than ordinary days but at the same time are occasions for deeper reflection,

are more charged with emotion and with the desire to engage in dialogue with the community outside, so that behind the walls more human doorways can continually be constructed to lead us back to society, to our families, to our children and to hope. So this feast of Mary, Mother of Christ, invites us to reflect on our being women and mothers.

I find this a very beautiful idea – while reflecting on Mary to reflect on who we are; to reflect on yourselves as baptized and consecrated women, women who are living out a call that concerns the whole of humanity.

It is true that we are poor men and women, and it is already a great deal if we succeed in living well from day to day, always trying to improve in what we are doing. But God has placed in Mary's heart the mystery of the world, and entering into Mary's heart we enter into this mystery. We make its dimensions our own, participating in the sufferings of all women on earth, even if we feel full of fear, infirmity, weakness and defects.

John Paul II in his apostolic exhortation, *Redemptionis Donum* (March 25, 1984) writes to religious:

> If the entire Church finds in Mary her first model, all the more reason do you find her so – you as consecrated individuals and communities within the Church! ... I address myself to you with this present message, to invite you to renew your religious consecration according to the model of the consecration of the very Mother of God... Persevering in fidelity to him who is faithful, strive to find a very special support in Mary! For she was called by God to the most perfect communion with his Son. May she, the faithful Virgin, also be

the Mother of your evangelical way: may she help you to experience and to show to the world how infinitely faithful is God himself! (17) (Vatican Polyglot Press).

Ask Mary, then, to open your heart to the vastness of your call, to the cosmic, universal and human meaning in which the religious experience is situated; to open your heart to receive the voices of all humanity.

A practical suggestion

My decision to limit the number of meditations was made for the sake of providing a certain contemplative space. Therefore a greater personal activity is needed between the meditations, and this activity should be programmed. I suggest three main points of emphasis: mental prayer, vocal prayer and spiritual reading.

It is important not to change the established plan without a valid, sensible reason.

– The material for mental prayer should be what is presented in the meditations. It ought to be taken up again in a personal contemplation that puts us in direct contact with the Lord. The actual basic fruit we are seeking is an encounter with the grace of the Holy Spirit, which springs from contemplating the mysteries of Jesus.

– For vocal prayer, besides the liturgy of the Mass, you might pray the Divine Office, the Way of the Cross and the rosary.

– For spiritual reading: the first two chapters of St Luke's gospel and chapters 19 and 20 of St John's. In some way they concur and are both dominated by the Marian theme. I also recommend your reading *Redemptionis Donum,* the encyclical *Marialis Cultus* by Pope Paul VI and chapter VIII of *Lumen Gentium.* Biographies or autobiographies of the saints could likewise be useful and, of course, it would be good to read from the Rules and Constitutions of your institute.

What is important is not the volume of reading but a definite programme, because solitude is difficult and requires rigorous interior discipline.

Now we shall conclude this introduction by reading the gospel passage which, as I said, will remain the fundamental point of reference of all our meditations:

> But standing by the cross of Jesus were his mother, and his mother's sister, Mary the wife of Clopas, and Mary Magdalene. When Jesus saw his mother, and the disciple whom he loved standing near, he said to his mother, "Woman, behold, your son!" Then he said to the disciple, "Behold, your mother!" And from that hour the disciple took her into his own home (Jn 19:25-27).

"Lord Jesus, we want to stand by your cross in union with your Mother. Grant us the grace of contemplation so that we can contemplate the meaning of this event and of all the events it contains.

Mary, Mother of Jesus, you understood the magnitude of your universal vocation. Help us to understand the breadth, vastness and immensity of our call.

We ask this of you, Father, through your crucified Son in union with Mary. Amen."

THE THREE GROANINGS

The Canaanite woman (Mt 15:21-28)

We shall begin this meditation by attempting to explain what it means to know the magnitude of a vocation. St Paul comes to our assistance in a passage from the Letter to the Romans:

> I consider that the sufferings of this present time are not worth comparing with the glory that is to be revealed to us. For the creation waits with eager longing for the revealing of the sons of God; for the creation was subjected to futility, not of its own will but by the will of him who subjected it in hope; because the creation itself will be set free from its bondage to decay and obtain the glorious liberty of the children of God. We know that the whole creation has been groaning in travail together until now; and not only the creation, but we ourselves, who have the first fruits of the Spirit, groan inwardly as we wait for adoption as sons, the redemption of our bodies. For in this hope we were saved. Now hope that is seen is not hope. For who hopes for what he sees? But if we hope for what we do not see, we wait for it with patience.
> Likewise the Spirit helps us in our weakness; for we do not know how to pray as we ought, but the Spirit himself intercedes for us with sighs too deep for words. And he who searches the hearts of men knows what is the mind of the Spirit, because the Spirit intercedes for the saints according to the will of God (Rom 8:18-27).

In this very beautiful text, the Apostle develops for us what we might call the "doctrine of the three groanings". What is a groan? It is a restrained cry, something connected with a certain kind of suffering. There is an inner urge to cry out, but the flow of air is blocked, as it were, and only a part of the cry is emitted. This, then, is characteristic of a groan: it is a cry that is violent in origin but subdued in expression.

Scripture speaks of groans. There are two important occurences in particular. The first is the groaning of Jesus as related by the evangelist:

> They brought to him a man who was deaf and had an impediment in his speech; and they besought him to lay his hand upon him. And taking him aside from the multitude privately, he put his fingers into his ears, and he spat and touched his tongue; and looking up to heaven, *he sighed,* and he said to him, *"Ephphatha,"* that is, "Be opened!" (Mk 7:32-34).

In Greek the verb is "groaned." So, in performing this miracle Jesus experiences a moment of severe spiritual tension. He thinks of humanity incapable of expressing itself, of this man who feels the need of communicating, and he puts into the healing of the deaf mute his whole will to save and at the same time the suffering of the man who cannot communicate. Jesus' groaning is a vehement participation in human suffering.

Another interesting passage occurs in the Acts (7:34) where direct reference is made to the words of Exodus: "I have seen the affliction of my people who are in Egypt, and I have heard their *cry...* and I have come down to deliver them out of the hand of the Egyptians" (cf. Ex 3:7-8).

Here too, the Greek text of the author of Acts uses the term "groan". "Groan" because it is a yearning for liberty that, given the circumstances of slavery in which the people live, cannot be expressed. The intensity of sentiment appears outwardly in a restrained, delicate form.

The groaning of creation

The first groaning is that of all creation:

> The creation waits with eager longing for the revealing of the sons of God... We know that the whole creation has been groaning in travail together until now (cf. vv. 19-22).

This is a grandiose image describing the dynamism of human history: it is all a groaning, like an immense labour pain. The word used in the Greek text *(sustenàzei)* means a groaning-with. The whole world groans together; it is a prodigious amount of pain. Humanity, history, creation aspire to something other and desire it immensely, long for it intensely. This cry for freedom in the heart of the world does not, however, succeed in expressing itself clearly, and although it is most profound, it turns out to be a mere groan.

Note the beauty of expression: "The whole creation has been groaning in travail." It is at a point in which life is about to be manifested by means of pain and suffering. We all know how the image of labour pains that are preparing for new life can be applied to the most intimate sufferings of a person, giving them meaning.

Humanity today is like the people of Israel when they were slaves of the Pharaoh of Egypt. We are slaves of non-sense, of an empty life and of stupidity. Slaves are people who ask what use there is in living, what sense in our worries and works. Slaves are those who live thoughtlessly without a purpose or who rapidly pass from thoughtlessness to despondency, anger and frustration.

Groaning expresses the need for meaning and the will to find the profound significance of things. Consequently humanity groans because it desires at all costs to be liberated from an empty life, from slavery to idols (drugs, looting, various forms of violence, hunger, abortion, exploitation).

And Christians as such are called to perceive the groaning of creation, to attune their ears to it, precisely because it is a groan, which is rarely expressed in clamorous tones and must therefore be sensed, much like a night nurse becomes aware of the groaning of a patient who no longer has the strength to cry out.

Our groaning

> We ourselves, who have the first fruits of the Spirit, groan inwardly as we wait for the adoption as sons, the redemption of our bodies (v. 23).

Although we have the first fruits of the Spirit, and even just because we already have a small foretaste of what it is to be saved from non-sense, frustration and futility, we ourselves as Christians groan, knowing that salvation is not yet complete. Our groans are our deepest, genuine desires that tend towards liberation or, as the Apostle says, *to our being God's children,* to becoming fully what we are. We are children of God, and yet we often live in a state of ignorance, minimal awareness, indolence and mediocrity; we are enveloped in our fragility and in all our opaqueness. We want our sonship, our daughterhood to be revealed, so that we can really speak with God as Father, as a Thou who loves us and saves us.

As St Paul adds, we want "our bodies to be set free". We desire to be freed from carnality as a burden in order to experience corporality as a gift. It is a long, slow and difficult journey. I have always been struck by a statement of St Thérèse of the Child Jesus made in an exhausted state during the latter days of her sufferings prior to her death: "My body has always been a nuisance to me, I do not feel comfortable in it... As a very small child I was ashamed of it" (*Novissima Verba*, July 30). These words show how this young woman, who had inwardly arrived at a state of perfect self-oblation, felt that she had still not fully integrated into it the entire reality of her bodiliness. It is an integration requiring a high degree of spiritual maturity, normally realized only in the course of a long life.

John Paul II has said very beautiful things about corporality as a symbol and spousal sign. But who is really able to live it? So there is the groaning under the burden of bodiliness, expressed as distress, temptation, sensuality, obtuseness of mind, inability to place ourselves truly at the disposition of others in forgetfulness of self.

These groanings which stir within us are important as signs of the Spirit within us, living in us and causing us to tend towards what we do not yet have but which gives meaning to our journey.

> Likewise the Spirit helps us in our weakness...
> himself intercedes for us with sighs too deep for
> words (v. 26).

Our groanings can be expressed in some way or
other, and we have tried to say something about
their content. It is impossible, however, to explain
the groanings of the Spirit, who cries out within us
and shows us how to pray. Nevertheless, when we
do succeed in perceiving this voice of the Spirit,
our groans too are purified and refined.

By means of the discipline of prayer, we ought
to detect the groanings of creation, of our people,
in harmony with the inexpressible groanings of the
Spirit. They are most lofty and most profound but
can be basically summarized, as Paul makes us
understand, in the word "Father!" which we learn
to say in the very power of the Spirit with increasing truth, peace, surrender, tenderness and confidence.

To know or to recover the magnitude of our
vocation means to listen to these three great
groanings, to discern them within us and to make
room for them. The breadth of our vocation is co-
extensive with these groans and not confined to
our own petty, limited personal groaning.

"The woman among her people" is every woman
capable of understanding with Mary the groanings
of all humanity, of expressing them within herself
and bringing them into accord with those of the
Spirit.

The Canaanite woman

The first gospel scene that we want to dwell on is that of the Canaanite woman, because it expresses and exemplifies the ability to listen to these groanings. It is a splendid episode which we can use to confront our life and our attitudes:

> Jesus went away from there and withdrew to the region of Tyre and Sidon. And behold, a Canaanite woman from that region came out and cried, "Have mercy one me, O Lord, Son of David; my daughter is severely possessed by a demon." But he did not answer her a word. And his disciples came and begged him, saying, "Send her away, for she is crying after us." He answered, "I was sent only to the lost sheep of the house of Israel." But she came and knelt before him, saying, "Lord, help me." And he answered, "It is not fair to take the children's bread and throw it to the dogs." She said, "Yes, Lord, yet even the dogs eat the crumbs that fall from their masters' table." Then Jesus answered her, "O woman, great is your faith! Be it done for you as you desire." And her daughter was healed instantly (Mt 15:21-28).

I suggest three reflections:

a) *The people.* The initial lines of the text refer to the people to whom the woman belongs. The Canaanites are the traditional enemies of the Chosen People, who drove them out on account of their cruel and savage paganism. They represented the residue of an ancient, depraved paganism.

Moreover, it is noted that this woman came from that "region", the territories of Tyre and Sidon, which convey the idea of triumphant, proud cities. The mention of "Canaanite" could indicate a coarse, popular, rural paganism, while Tyre and Sidon suggest a picture of arrogance, of cities boastful of their power, metropolises without God.

This woman comes, therefore, from a very dark environment, from a humanity immersed in nonsense, in futility and slavery to idols. We can say that she comes from our people, for all of us are part of a humanity lacking meaning and searching for the right direction, in need of true and lasting values.

b) *The daughter.* Behind this woman, her daughter emerges: "My daughter is possessed by a demon." It is strange that she says, "my daughter," and not "our daughter". Probably this mother is alone, a widow, or the father has run off and abandoned her, just because of this daughter who makes life impossible. In any case, we are faced a desolate woman.

What does it mean to be "possessed by a demon"? We do not know the details of the illness, but it was certainly a case of strong psychic depression. The devil is a vicious reality that leads to discouragement. The girl throws herself on the ground, weeps continuously, does not want to talk to anyone, and nothing is right with her. She is a person who becomes an insupportable burden beyond all help. Each of us has known such cases – people who complain about everything, never sleep well, always get bad food and put the blame on one annoyance after another.

Perhaps even more is contained in the expression, "possessed by a demon," for example, what we read in the episode of the lunatic boy (Mt 17:14-23): the inclination to make trouble for oneself and for others. I can think of families I have known in which mothers are veritable prisoners of a son or daughter who even strikes them. Yet the mothers always excuse their children, try to conceal and hide the situation from others and sometimes become obsessive about doting on these sick children. We can imagine this woman being like this with her daughter.

c) *The woman.* As mother and woman, I think we could describe this Canaanite with three qualities: She identifies herself with her daughter, she is intrepid and she is sure.

— *Identified:* She could have considered her life as separate from that of her daughter, but instead she identifies with her to a degree that the evangelist expresses in very subtle terms: "Have mercy on *me, my daughter* is possessed..." She is asking mercy for herself but in reality she is requesting it for her daughter. And in her insistence she exclaims, "Lord, help me!" She does not say: "Help my daughter." In this situation she experiences perfect union with her daughter.

Jesus replies, "Woman, great is your faith. Be it done for you as you desire." He does not speak of a cure, because the woman has become so much one with her daughter's groanings that to grant her petition is to heal her daughter.

— *Bravery:* She is not at all resentful and pursues her daughter's cause with a devotion that knows no discouragement. We could have thought that since she was at the end of her resources, after Jesus' silence she would have had to say, "That's it! He didn't even listen to me. I'd better stop." Instead, with extraordinary strength of soul she insists, and even when Jesus gives her a harsh answer she continues with admirable tenacity, humility and patience. She has lovingly espoused her cause – in this sense she is a perfect woman! – and will not give up for any reason.

– *She is sure of Jesus* and trusts him. She is a woman who has gone through "the ford of faith". That is, she does not let her faith depend on passing gratifications – whether Jesus answers her kindly, meets her halfway, is attentive to her. She is so sure of Jesus that she remains firm and, therefore, as we shall see, she is an image of Mary at the wedding in Cana.

Here we naturally ask ourselves: "How is it that this Canaanite woman, coming as she does from an dark civilization, living in the shadow of Tyre and Sidon, cities traditionally closed to heaven, has such faith?" There is no doubt, in fact, that she has attained the highest peak of gospel faith. By identifying herself with her daughter's suffering, the Canaanite has become humble, poor, and at heart has already abandoned the dark regions of diffidence, the mists of arrogance and pride. She is a woman redeemed by daily life and mellowed by her day-to-day sufferings until she has attained the perfection of confidence of the "little ones" for whom the gospel is self-evident.

In conclusion, let us ask ourselves:

Who is this daughter? In the daughter we recognize something of ourselves – our moodiness, our ill-humour, our inner bad temper, our discontent, our allowing Satan's fumes and darkness to gain the upper hand at times. We are this daughter when we are full of gossip, mistrust, quarrelsomeness, sulkiness.

Modern people are also like this daughter. They are dissatisfied with themselves, and their groanings spring not from hope but from rage, desperation and scepticism.

Who is this mother? We can check ourselves for the attitudes on which we have reflected. Each of us can ask ourselves:

– *How do I identify myself* with the burdensome situations entrusted to me?

I ought to identify with them in a spirit of dedication, not possessively, as though managing them like personal property.

The question is not to realize yourselves either as women or as religious, but in virtue of your consecration to serve the people entrusted to your care, above all in humanly difficult and sad situations.

– *Am I brave?* Never resentful, always resolved to serve at all costs, to find the positive solution, never giving up or losing courage, never letting myself be seized by vexation or anger?

– *Am I sure of Jesus?* Have I crossed the "ford of faith," or do I instead continually ask myself whether the Lord loves me, helps me, whether he is near or has forgotten me? Beyond immediate consolations, even in prayer, do I live – in profound, intimate conviction of Jesus – the groaning of the Spirit who says, "Father!" and says it incessantly?

These are the questions that the Canaanite woman suggests to us so that we may truly learn to become mothers of this humanity, to live the consecrated life as a motherhood for the world and its people, thus participating in Mary's motherhood.

MARY HEEDS THE WORLD'S GROANINGS

The wedding at Cana (Jn 2:1-12)

"O Mary, we contemplate you beside the cross of Jesus, identified with his pain just as the Canaanite woman identified herself with the pain and suffering of her daughter! We see you courageous, imperturbable like the Canaanite, so much so that you can receive at this moment a universal mission, and your personal sorrow leads you to share in all the world's suffering, including our own. Teach us, Mary, how to identify with your Son in his pain and in that of the world and how to be courageous like you by the grace of the Holy Spirit, which we invoke upon ourselves from the Father in Jesus' name. Amen."

The wedding at Cana

The gospel scene on which we shall now meditate presents Mary, who listens to the groaning of the world and in so doing enters even more deeply into the inner dispositions of the Canaanite woman.

> On the third day there was a marriage at Cana in Galilee, and the mother of Jesus was there; Jesus also was invited to the marriage, with his disciples. When the wine failed, the mother of Jesus said to him, "They have no wine." And Jesus said to her, "O woman, what have you to do with me? My hour has not yet come." His mother said to the

servants, "Do whatever he tells you." Now six stone jars were standing there, for the Jewish rites of purification, each could hold twenty or thirty gallons. Jesus said to them, "Fill the jars with water." And they filled them up to the brim. He said to them, "Now draw some out and take it to the steward of the feast." So they took it. When the steward of the feast tasted the water now become wine, and did not know where it came from (though the servants who had drawn the water knew) the steward of the feast called the bridegroom and said to him, "Every man serves the good wine first and when men have drunk freely, then the poor wine; but you have kept the best wine until now." This, the first of Jesus' signs, Jesus did at Cana in Galilee, and manifested his glory; and his disciples believed in him. After this he went down to Capernaum with his mother and his brethren and his disciples; and there they stayed for a few days (Jn 2:1-12).

This text is rich in mystery. We need only notice how it begins:

On the third day. These words have a profound resonance in the New Testament. The third day is the day of the resurrection, the day when glory was fully revealed. In this case it is also the third day of a great week, the week in which Jesus first revealed himself.

There was a marriage. A fact that is made so evident ought to lead to reflection. A great religious poet of our times, who sings of Mary, writes:

> We do well to note how the entire gospel is an invitation to a wedding feast. "The kingdom of heaven may be compared to a king who gave a marriage feast for his son" (Mt 22:2). The Church celebrates the Incarnation itself as a nuptial banquet of God with the whole of nature. And for Israel,

even the relationship between Yahweh and the people was sung as a sublime marriage, the synthesis of every other human love. Christ too speaks of the end of the world in the form of a nuptial meeting... Jesus himself is the bridegroom; and the entire Church is a bride awaiting the return of the beloved.

(Davide M. Turoldo, *Non hanno più vino*, Queriniana 1979, pp. 153-154.)

These words enable us to understand what is evoked by John's mysterious language when he mentions a wedding as a first episode and in so doing makes the mystery of Christ emerge in this very human reality.

The mother of Jesus was there. Mary is at the centre of this narrative. Even Jesus and his disciples appear in a rather subdued light: "Jesus *also* was invited with his disciples." For the evangelist the person of the mother is undoubtedly central, and it is from her that attention is cast on Jesus. The miracle, the manifestation of Christ's glory, passes through the mother.

In a certain sense, the significance and depth of the symbols contained in this passage defy any attempt to express them in words. So I invite you to relish it in contemplation, letting yourself be inwardly moved by the power of the Spirit. I limit myself to underlining some points that more specifically concern our meditation, and propose these three: 1) Mary's perception of the whole; 2) Mary's involvement; 3) Mary's courage.

Mary's perception of the whole

Let us begin with a very beautiful quote from St Thérèse of the Child Jesus in her auto-biography where she speaks of her childhood:

> Although I was lively by nature, I could not hurl myself into the usual games for children of my age; even during recreation, I would lean against a tree and in this position contemplate *everything at a glance*, abandoning myself to serious reflection! (*Manuscript A*, 115)

This passage gives a splendid picture of the characteristic that Mary displayed at the wedding feast in Cana.

In the gospel account, everyone has something to do – some in the kitchen, others serving and still others playing musical instruments. Only Mary sees the whole, can take in everything at a glance and recognizes what is essentially taking place and where essential things are lacking. This is Mary's contemplative spirit, her gift of synthesis, the ability to notice details. Certainly she too had some material service to render. Nevertheless she paid attention to every detail and, as though leaning on a tree – to use St Thérèse's expression – she contemplated the whole and sized up the situation.

The gift of synthesis is typically feminine. It is the ability to see the core of a matter with the understanding of the heart and not by means of reasoning or direct, prompt analysis of all the constituent elements.

Mary perceives the world's unexpressed groaning and expresses it simply: *"They have no wine."* She is the only one who says this. Probably others also noticed it, but as though in reverie. They see that something is running out and not knowing what to do about it they prefer to go on, feigning ignorance.

The grace of your vocation as consecrated persons consists precisely in cultivating, even in individual duties, an eye for the whole in situations that concern the community, the group, the Church and society, so that you can lovingly notice difficult, delicate moments, give them a voice and take discreet, effective steps to help.

Every religious ought to desire this marvellous contemplative gift. It is not expertise or dexterity in some area or other, or specialization in a human ability, but a comprehensive perception that knows how to preserve a sense of the whole. Though this may be difficult to express in words, it is important, even necessary, for the Church's life. It includes the gift of governing, of effective action, of careful programming; it is a "Petrine" charism basic to the functioning of the ecclesial body. The contemplative charism is something subtler and more indefinable that lends unity, gusto, savour and consistency to the Church as a whole. It is the charism of Mary, and if it were lacking, the Church would be threatened with becoming a society of experts, proficients and specialists, in which each one championed his or her own particular ideal, perhaps disputing with others in the name of personal competence.

Mary's charism is the comforting glance at the entire ecclesial body which renders her attentive to all the sore spots and prompt to give them expression and to assist by advising one person as to what should be done and another as to the means of intervention. At Cana Mary does not provide directly when wine is needed but brings the need to light, puts it in relief and entrusts it to her Son. The following verses express this very nicely:

> Now a song arises from our heart
> like a gift offered to you, O Mother:
> You persuaded your Son to work
> his first sign at the wedding in Cana.
> Caringly you said, "They have no more wine."
> Since then, your eye is the first to see
> joy disappearing from our feasts,
> but now you know and can command.
>
> (Davide M. Turoldo, *Non abbiamo più vino*,
> "Laudario alla Vergine," EDB 1980, p. 74.)

Let us, then, ask the Blessed Virgin to watch over our feasts, the feast that is our community, our local Church, the Church in our country and the universal Church. And also to keep an eye on the feast that is our society and to make us attentive to what is lacking, to instill in us the contemplative, benevolent, sincere glance with which she surveyed the feasting during the wedding celebration at Cana. Let us petition Mary not to allow our heart to fret over small private trivialities but to make our heart beat in unison with the great banquet of human life, noticing and interpreting the situation of all those who have no wine, bread or joy and are not involved in the banquet.

Each one of us can ask ourselves: "Am I so preoccupied with my personal charge and my work that I no longer have any enthusiasm for the life of the community, the Church and society at large? Am I so tenacious and insistent in pursuing my own particular assignment that I no longer realize that it ought to be integrated into the whole of a well-spread table in which all share with love and joy? Am I so little contemplative that I see only the trees and overlook the forest?"

34

Mary's involvement

Mary could have contented herself with her contemplative gesture. If she had, she would not have demonstrated the tenacity of the Canaanite woman that identifies itself with the situation. She would have revealed something and made a sociological, statistical analysis without entering into the problem. Instead, Mary entered into it so intimately as to merit a kind of rebuke from Jesus. They are the mysterious words on which scholars have written volumes without, however, arriving at a consensus regarding their exact meaning: *"Woman, what have you to do with me?"*

This is certainly not an encouraging expression, regardless of what meaning we try to attribute to it. Mary accepts it because she is involved in the situation as though it were her own: "They have no wine" means *we* have no more wine. It means identifying herself with these poor people, whose name we do not even know and about whom the gospel account does not tell us anything else. Two more stanzas of the above-mentioned poem help us to penetrate Mary's state of soul:

> Yes, we do not have any more wine, Mother!
> Our loves are joyless,
> our fortune grace-less
> and even our feasts no longer know faith!
> For her faith in Christ's hour,
> we render you, Father, glory.
> Satiate us with that other wine of your Son,
> he wine of the Spirit, our inebriation.
> (Davide M. Turoldo, *ibid.*)

The fact that wine should run out at a banquet is not actually so important. The guests would have gone home just as satisfied. Hence the shortage that Mary notices is not essential, not a matter of life or death. It is a lack of *well-being,* that *certain something* which makes things work well, and it is just this which is often lacking to us. Frequently we are devoid of that *I-don't-know-what* in the way of joy, enthusiasm and fervour needed to make things run smoothly. How many communities are deficient in this wine! The essentials of the religious life are there: the vows are kept, the offices are fulfilled with attention and seriousness, external works are accomplished to the satisfaction of the people. And yet there is lacking that "certain something" represented by the wine!

To discover this is a grace that the consecrated community ought to ask of our Lady, because it does not result merely from the sociological analyses that we undertake. To the famous question of why there is a falling-off of vocations we usually answer in various ways: we have not updated sufficiently, we have updated too much; we have remained closed, we have been too open; we have kept the habit, we have abandoned it. In reality it is not easy to express what counts most, even though on visiting a religious community it may become evident that here – notwithstanding the inevitable defects – *there is wine!*

Mary must help us to detect what is missing, not in order to accuse or recriminate but in order to suffer and to love. Above all, she must help me to discover what is lacking in myself, that *certain something* which produces the extra. Perhaps my deficiencies are slight: small steps that I should take in disciplining body, spirit and mind; small acts of pardon and small renunciations to be experienced; small tensions to be eased or small words to be checked. Maybe I only need a little in order to make the good wine appear.

The evangelist stresses the quality of the wine three times: "Every man serves the *good* wine first and when men have drunk freely, then the poor wine. But you have kept the *best* wine until now." Wine can be real wine and yet not good, whether on account of the quality of the grapes or the lack of skill in preparation. Jesus wants that good wine, the product of the richness derived from the combin-ation of grapes, sun, heat, soil, preparation and decanting. He wants it for our life, for the full growth of our communities and for the joy of woman in the Church and in society.

The good wine that Jesus desires is likewise the radiation of charisms, of vitality and of readiness for service on the part of all the baptized and in particular of all women in the Church.

Jesus' wine at Cana knows no measure, it is *abundant*: "Six stone jars... each could hold twenty or thirty gallons," filled to the brim. Our spiritual life, perhaps marked by dryness or fatigue, ought to be deep down a gushing wine, the superabun-dance of the Spirit nourishing us day and night and never running out. It should not be merely a residue in the bottom of the glass that can scarcely quench anyone's thirst!

Mary's courage

Jesus does not say that he will provide, but Mary says to the waiters, "Do whatever he tells you." Her words have a time-tested biblical sense, as it were. They are in fact the words pronounced by Pharaoh during the famine in Egypt when the people had

nothing: "'Go to Joseph; what he says to you, do.'
There was famine in all lands. Then Joseph opened
all storehouses" (Gen 41:55-56). Here Mary appears in the light of the man who satisfied the
hunger of an entire country. Mary is she through
whom Jesus' power is manifested on earth for all
of humanity. She is *sure* of her son because he is
the Son of God.

This is perhaps the conviction which comes to
us least easily. Though we may become aware that
wine is lacking, though we may identify ourselves
rather sadly with the dryness of our life, of our
community and of our local Churches, we nevertheless do not succeed in crossing the "ford of
faith". We remain at a standstill, bitterly considering the situation or seeking inadequate solutions.

Sometimes when I hear certain analyses and
evaluations, for example, regarding the dearth of
vocations, I have the impression that remedies are
proposed without conviction. Remedies are needed
and programmes are necessary. We have to do
something, but that is not the *conviction about
Jesus* which alone gives power to all our action.
Our faith is insufficient; we are wanting in that
qualitative leap which consists not in looking for
the key to the hidden treasure but rather in *security
in Jesus* even in the simplest matters, in the most
ordinary expressions of consecrated life.

All of us can ask ourselves:
— How can I imitate Mary, leaving it to the Spirit
to arouse in me the grace of synthesis, the gift of
seeing the whole?
— How can I participate in Mary's involvement?
— How can I attain her courage, which is total
confidence in Christ?

The answer is not easy because it presupposes a full gospel life. There is, however, an important means, often overlooked – that of giving room for contemplation. We can approach Mary by means of prayerful reading of the word of God, reading Scripture in the Holy Spirit.

A theoretical study of what we read is not enough; it must be cultivated. Here, learning means selecting some aspects or words of the gospel passage and putting them into practice. But then the words should be re-read and compared with one another in imitation of Mary who "kept all these things in her heart" (cf. Lk 2:19.51). Mary is a model of involvement and courage because she is a *model of contemplation.* This is one of the secrets of consecrated life in the Church: to be a source of contemplation and to mould masters of prayer and contemplation that offer these dimensions of life to every Christian. I recall Thérèse of the Child Jesus who while still a child felt contemplation spring up in her when she observed nature (*Manuscript A,* 50). But teachers who have not experienced this gift of contemplation personally cannot cultivate or understand its presence in children.

The most pressing duty of consecrated persons is to cultivate contemplation and to make it accessible to others; to make society recognize the primacy of contemplation over action, of existence over work and of being over having.

"O Mary, help us to arrive at the heart of your contemplative existence in the Church!"

THE FORD OF FAITH

Homily
1st Reading: Ez 28:1-10; 2nd Reading: Mt 19:23-30

The two readings of the liturgy present two aspects of the country from which the Canaanite woman came, the country of Canaan or of Tyre and Sidon. It was the situation of darkness and sin common to each of us as members of the human race. By God's mercy, we have been called from this situation to salvation. Nevertheless we remain largely bound by this situation throughout our lives.

By virtue of baptism and of the religious vows, consecrated life is the gradual exit from the land of origin in which we are born and live. The biblical texts show us two characteristics typical of the environment of sin in which humanity finds itself.

The *first text* (Ez 28:1-10) highlights arrogance and pride under the name of the prince of Tyre. The passage belongs to a series of prophecies against the nations which offer a gloomy picture of human reality.

The *second text* (Mt 19:23-30) treats the theme of possessions and riches.

1. *A first observation.* Both readings emphasize vices and negative conduct that is more specifically masculine than feminine. Pride and the desire for power are typical of the man. In the woman they are perhaps expressed as vanity, the desire to be important to someone, to be praised and admired. All the same, it is another form of the same basic tendency of pride.

41

The spirit of possessiveness, the urge to accumulate money as such, likewise belongs to man. To woman, money is valuable as a means of buying clothes, jewellery and nice things. These are reciprocal and complementary aspects of the same reality.

But I want to make an observation. It is true that for the woman these fundamental deviations of the human spirit are manifested as vanity, desire for praise and the possibility of ostentation. When, however, we pass from individuals to associations, groups and communities, these defects pose a threat for the communities themselves in a very specific way. There is a group of arrogance and pride and a group of spirit of possession that seriously corrodes even Orders and Congregations of religious women. Personally we live in poverty, humility and detachment, but it seems that this is not valid for the community, for – as they say – business is business and prudence is necessary.

In a certain sense this is true; nevertheless I am always particularly edified by those religious communities that live out a collective humility, are detached from money and possessions and give witness to real simplicity of life.

We should realize that holiness and the journey out of the land of Canaan are required of the community and not only of the individual. Consequently superiors are called upon to reflect on this and to defend the poverty of the group from the criticism of those who consider it right to accumulate or retain goods and money. Of course discernment in this matter is not always easy.

2. *A second observation.* In these Scripture readings the descriptions of the deviations seem at

first sight rather excessive, and we are tempted to think that they deal with things that do not happen to us. It would never occur to us to boast to the point of claiming, "I am a god," or of thinking ourselves "divinely enthroned far out to sea". We conclude, therefore, that the reading does not concern us.

So I suggest two applications that can strike home:

– In the personal life of a religious, what corresponds to this proud proclamation attributed to the prince of Tyre? If finds its parallel in not having crossed "the ford of faith", in not yet decisively left it to God to determine my life project the direction of my life. What is pride in Ezekiel and could be outwardly manifested as a kind of vanity and showiness in a woman becomes inwardly an attachment and clinging to my own life plan. This includes plans for the tasks entrusted to me, at times on the professional level, and plans of spiritual progress and unconscious hopes to which I cling tenaciously, not really accepting the fact that God acts upon me and with me in a very different way. I would like to be different, without my limitations or defects, and this wishful thinking, marked by impatience and resentment, keeps me discontented with myself and with others, preventing me from devoting myself to asceticism of body and spirit. This means not to have passed through the ford of faith. At times this failure to cross the ford of faith manifests itself in regret at having pursued a path, in the hope of something or other, only to discover that things have turned out differently. I feel disillusioned with myself and with the community, and rather than taking it as an occasion for abandoning myself to God's plans, I fall into desolation, melancholy, resentment and various kinds of neuroses.

On the spiritual journey, all this could correspond to the incredible pride of the prince of Tyre, who otherwise seems to far removed from our experience.

Now, what corresponds to the urge to possess, spoken of in our Gospel passage, which somehow seems not to concern us? I would say it is attachment to small things, which is easier than clinging to big things.

It is a spirit of possessiveness that becomes evident and usually increases with age, becoming an anxiety over the security to which we have become accustomed: the house, the environment in which we live, the circle of acquaintances and friends that form part of our apostolic commitment and are in reality a help for us personally. All this comes to be *our possession*, so much so that the very thought of being deprived of it strongly affects us and gives us a bad shake-up within. How many a drama connected with a transfer, for instance, is bound up with our being attached to the various things that make up our life! We need not be surprised at this, but it ought to be an alarm signal reminding us of how far we still are from truly giving ourselves. Worrying about this is of no use. What is more helpful is confidence in God's word: "With men this is impossible, but with God all things are possible." The miracle of the camel passing through the eye of a needle can also happen to us, even though it may seem that we are every bit as bulky as a camel, despite our having renounced so many things.

"With God all things are possible." These words recall great Marian themes because they were said in connection with the birth of John the Baptist and, therefore, associate us with the mystery of the Annunciation and of the Visitation. For God it is certainly possible to make my life, with all its bonds, pass through the eye of the needle of the mystery of the cross.

I need only be sure of Christ, trust in him and entrust myself to him, without presuming to have attained any degree of detachment.

"Lord, I entrust myself to you.
You know that I love you.
You know my weakness and fragility.
You know that, though I consider
myself detached,
I lament like a wounded eagle
if I am suddenly deprived of something
that I deem important.
You, Lord, will lead me with your strength
to go out of Egypt,
towards the conquest of the land of Canaan.
Mary, help me to look within myself
and at myself with the look of truth,
liberty, and simplicity
that will put me on the right road
of the cross and resurrection."

THE SPIRIT OF GOSPEL FAITH

The sinful woman in Simon's house (Lk 7:36-50)

"Mary, beside the cross you felt the extraordinary power of the redemption of man and woman vibrating in the tremors of the dying Jesus. Enable us also to feel this power, so that we can let it vibrate in our bodies and voices and transmit it to others who are called like us and with us to this mission."

Let us now spend some time in reflection near the cross, the heart of the redemption. We have already meditated on some of the ideal attitudes of woman, the woman who becomes involved in the sufferings of society, who bravely faces them and who brings into them a spirit of unshakable faith.

Now we want to deepen our spirit of faith in the redemption which makes us – sinful, weak and poor as we are – instruments of salvation.

The sinful woman in Simon's house

The Evangelist Luke is the narrator of our gospel scene:

> One of the Pharisees asked him to eat with him, and he went into the Pharisee's house, and sat at table. And behold, a woman of the city, who was a sinner, when she learned that he was sitting at table in the Pharisee's house, brought an alabaster flask of ointment, and standing behind him at his feet, weeping, she began to wet his feet with her

and kissed his feet, and anointed them with the ointment. Now when the Pharisee who had invited him saw it, he said to himself, "If this man were a prophet, he would have known who and what sort of woman this is who is touching him, for she is a sinner." And Jesus answering said to him, "Simon, I have something to say to you." And he answered, "What is it, Teacher?" "A certain creditor had two debtors; one owed five hundred denarii, and the other fifty. When they could not pay, he forgave them both. Now which of them will love him more?" Simon answered, "The one, I suppose, to whom he forgave more." And he said to him, "You have judged rightly." Then turning toward the woman he said to Simon, "Do you see this woman? I entered your house, you gave me no water for my feet, but she has wet my feet with her tears and wiped them with her hair. You gave me no kiss, but from the time I came in she has not ceased to kiss my feet. You did not anoint my head with oil, but she has anointed my feet with ointment. Therefore I tell you, her sins, which are many, are forgiven, for she loved much; but he who is forgiven little, loves little." And he said to her, "Your sins are forgiven." Then those who were at table with him began to say among themselves, "Who is this, who even forgives sins?" And he said to the woman, "Your faith has saved you; go in peace." (Lk 7:36-50)

This very beautiful episode is difficult to interpret because it is unusual in every part. Above all, it borders the limits of propriety, as it were. Just imagine something like this happening during a bishop's pastoral visit. What scandal it would cause among the people, and what spicy pictorial reports would circulate in the various weeklies! It is not by chance that only Luke recounts this scene.

It is difficult to grasp its actual, shocking meaning. Moreover, it is difficult because scholars do not agree on the translation of some words. For example, the famous sentence – *"Therefore, I tell you, her sins, which are many, are forgiven, for she loved much"* (v. 47) – is embarrassing. It would seem more logical to say: "Because she has loved much, her many sins have been forgiven her." Or: "Because many sins have been forgiven her, she shows love." As it is, however, the text is difficult to grasp in its precise import, leaving scholars and commentators perplexed as to where the accent falls. Even the conclusion – "Your faith has saved you" – represents a difficulty. Is the theme of this passage, then, love or faith? And how is it that faith suddenly turns up, whereas at first only love was mentioned?

Finally, this passage is difficult because in order to understand it a person would have to penetrate to the depths of the *"Planet Woman"*, to the woman's reactions and modes of expression, which often remain unknown. One thing is certain – Simon has not set foot on this planet and, therefore, does not understand anything. One would need the heart of Christ, for only he can enter into the "mystery" of the woman and comprehend the exact point of the situation despite the multiple, discordant evaluations of the event. As in the case of the other gospel scenes, I limit myself to a few general remarks about Simon, the woman and Jesus.

Simon

It is helpful to read the context immediately preceding our account. After having eulogized the Baptist, Jesus says:

For John the Baptist has come, not eating bread, not drinking wine, and you say, "He has a demon." The Son of man has come eating and drinking; and you say, 'Behold, a glutton and a drunkard, a friend of tax collectors and sinners!' Yet wisdom is justified by all her children" (vv. 33-35).

Evidently there were many divergent opinions about Jesus. Each one judged from his or her own point of view, and if that view was out of focus, the person could not understand Jesus and therefore did not do justice to wisdom. This is precisely what happened in Simon's house. Neither Simon nor his guests nor even the apostles understood Jesus. Only the woman, the daughter of wisdom, understood him. Now let us take a look at Simon.

1. Simon simply does not grasp what is happening. He is terrified and dismayed at the embarrassing situation created and at the bad figure he is cutting in the eyes of the other Pharisees. In inviting Jesus, he thought he had made a plucky gesture and was probably giving Jesus occasion for showing himself to be a wise, rigorous, grave and erudite teacher. Instead, his plan has snagged, and he is at a loss as to what to do. The rabbi is making a spectacle of himself before the guests; there is whispering, and the people in the room become restless. As a result, Simon is disconsolate. He would like to intervene but does not dare to, seeing that the master seems to be going along with the game. This too discourages him. Certainly, it would have been easy enough to say to the woman, "Out of here!" But it is beyond him.

He is a man very much wrapped up in himself, dissatisfied with what is going on around him but not in the least disposed to blame himself for it.

Instead, he regards himself as the ill-fated hero of the situation. He tried his best to pay honour to Jesus, to get him on friendly terms with important people who did not look on him with favour, and now his hopes are dashed to pieces. It does not occur to him to assume the least responsibility or guilt for it. Rather, he thinks he is the only one who has maintained a dignified appearance in this ticklish and difficult turn of events. So we can imagine his bewilderment when Jesus completely reverses the situation and accuses him. "How do you regard this woman, Simon?" To him she is like smoke in the eyes, playing as she does a negative social role. He despises her, and in his heart he also despises the naiveté of Jesus, who is not aware of being deceived, although he had seemed to possess so much common sense and such deep insight into people.

For Simon, this woman is merely an object to be removed, not to be given any attention. Not wanting to drive her away, he is waiting for her to go on her own so that the subject can finally be changed. Probably Simon pretends not to see the woman, to be occupied with something else. In reality his eyes are furiously following her, in the hope that she will stop.

2. Who is Simon? We are Simon every time we do not grasp the situation but evaluate it superficially without trying to penetrate it. We are Simon every time we judge others without mercy and so create much suffering. It is suffering that emerges in such an extremely delicate form from that booklet which I already mentioned having received from the women prisoners at St Victor's. The following sentence from it expresses well their

51

amazement at anyone's being concerned about them:

> So your visit moves us on this very day known to most as a holiday, a day off for relaxation. It moves us because we understand how important it is to you to dedicate time, attention and voice to this marginal place, perhaps among the more dramatic of our society. We wish to dedicate to you some voices, emotions, sorrows and joys of our being imprisoned women and mothers. They are certainly also dramatic moments from which we distance ourselves with difficulty, with pain and with maternal shame. But we entrust them to you, confident and filled with hope that to our mistakes there will not be added any mistakes on the part of society which could rebound upon the small band of children today and future generations tomorrow.

Of the three attributes – woman, mother and prisoner – Simon considers only the last. He supposes the sinful woman to be guilty, and that suffices. He does not regard her as woman or mother. It does not at all occur to him that the sinful woman could have a history: she is a woman, perhaps a mother, who has her problems and anxieties, has probably never received help from anyone and could have experienced moments of rallying. It does not even occur to him that this woman is making a generous effort. No, according to Simon she does not belong to the category of people who can improve.

This just man, because he is just and truly irreproachable, has manifested courage in inviting Jesus, but now shows that he does not understand anything at all. The drama of it is that many agree with Simon, and the people round about who hear about the banquet probably say, "The poor man!

For his generosity, Simon was put into a fine mess! Jesus of Nazareth should not have let that happen!"

As I have already said, however, Simon is not dead but is alive in us. He lives in our society with his virtues, his merits, his respectability, but likewise with his non-gospel obtuseness, with which he even dares to lay down the law for Jesus: "If he knew; if he were really a prophet!" There are authoritarian lay people who say: "If the Church were conscious of her responsibility she would understand what she is doing!"

We are Simon every time we fail to accuse ourselves and to question ourselves about what we are doing wrong and instead rush to judge others – including Jesus and including the Church – without leaving aside our rigidity and the good individual and collective consciousness of being all right.

The woman

What does the woman see and do? Above all she sees rightly; she possesses that sense of the whole which we contemplated in Mary at Cana. There in the bustle of the wedding feast Mary noticed what was beginning to run out; here in the bustle of the banquet and the chatter, this woman sees that Jesus has not been appropriately honoured. She has grasped the essence of the situation and has had the intuition of contemplative synthesis. The retaining of this contemplative synthesis which springs from the understanding of the heart is, as we have already said, of fundamental importance for the welfare of the Church and of society.

In addition, this woman does what she can and knows how to do. She does it with her whole being, even beyond what is reasonable. What she does is certainly excessive when viewed in itself (such things do not happen at every banquet) and approaches the limits of propriety. Less would have sufficed, had she wanted to obtain something or simply rehabilitate herself. But she wants to express that which she feels is lacking to Jesus and what Jesus deserves. She acts beyond all calculation. She has comprehended that Christ is beyond all and one can, therefore, never do enough for him; there are no rules or limits, because he is all and claims all.

In her intuition of faith, the woman naturally reviews her history, her life, her sins, her mistakes. But from what she has heard about Jesus and from his way of acting and his glance – probably she met him a few times in the street – she has caught a reflection of God's *heséd,* his tender mercy, and now she wants to praise with all her might this merciful tenderness, the only thing that can understand and save her.

That is what she does and experiences: the discovery of mercy in a real person. She feels ecstasy, self-transcendence, freedom of spirit, joy, unconcern about the others and disregard of their judgements and grumblings: all that springs precisely from discovering the love of Jesus.

Jesus

Jesus remains calm. Without becoming restless, he quietly evaluates the good aspect of the situation in that contemplative clarity that is part and parcel of his ordinary life. He perceives that the woman has understood, that she has thrown herself at his feet with love, that she is experiencing the ecstacy of mercy, and now he turns the tables. He turns to Simon and with a subtle discourse, full of humour, making of him a teacher as it were pins hin down. Simon realizes that he has blundered completely; he becomes aware that his presumption and self-sufficiency have rendered him more obtuse than this woman. Jesus, however, reproaches him with love and lovingly leads him to recognize that he has not justified wisdom, has not shown himself to be a child of wisdom.

Then he also explains the woman's excessive manner of acting. He does not interpret it by saying, "Yes, she is an exaggerated woman, a bit disturbed." He gives a theological explanation, "Her sins, which are many, are forgiven." It is a theology that penetrates to the depths of the truth of this woman; it does not excuse or cover up anything: it re-establishes perfect truth, without connivance or indulgence toward sin, along the line of mercy and rehabilitation.

Finally Jesus praises faith: "Your faith has saved you." This woman has crossed the ford of faith, and it is worthwhile to explain this expression again in more detail in the light of this gospel account. By ford is meant a decisive crossing, a moment in which a person makes a decision that overcomes a previous uncertainty and casts himself into an undertaking from which there is no turning back. Other expressions for the same thing could be: to burn the bridges or sink the ships.

Perhaps one of the best known examples of this crossing in Scripture is that of the ford of the Jabbok where Jacob wrestled all night with the angel (cf. Gen 32:23-32). Likewise the crossing of the Jordan with Joshua to enter the promised land is a ford of faith, because the people invests itself and risks everything. Abraham's setting out and then ascending Mount Moriah is also a ford of faith.

It always concerns decisive crossings in which the word "faith" underlines the ethical aspect, that of trust, and not so much the fundamental, cognitive aspect – the faith of the Credo – whose ford is baptism followed by the profession of faith that the child pronounces when it has reached the age of reason. In fact, by the "faith of Abraham" we mean the totality of his life of self-surrender to God and not solely his belief that God is great and provident. Both of these aspects must be integrated.

In other words, it is the *spirit of faith*, of becoming imbued on one's journey as believer with a total dedication of self to the God of revelation, a dedication that becomes increasingly spontaneous and integrated into the person's actual experience. Nor is that all. By the spirit of faith could also be meant Adam's faith before he sinned. Adam certainly relied on the gratuitous divine gift, praised God and lived the humility of one who recognizes that everything comes from his Creator and Father.

The ford of faith is the spirit of gospel faith: that of the publican who acknowledges the freedom of the pardon offered to the sinner by Jesus crucified. This and only this, is mature faith, which the redeemed sinner lives in an attitude of compunction, supplication and intercession before God's mercy. At times we do not attentively consider our condition as pardoned sinners always in need of pardon again. Then we rely on our praising God and recognizing his primacy, like Adam did. Such acts are right, necessary and important but not yet rooted in our historical condition as sinners. So we can say that the ninety-nine just who feel dispensed from doing penance are not worth as much in God's sight as one soul that lives in the compunction of the publican or of the sinful woman.

That is the faith which Jesus praises in the woman: *"Your faith has saved you."* Sometimes we could think we have already taken an important step because we have acknowledged the truth of Jesus Christ, whereas we have not yet set out on the path toward maturity in the spirit of penitent gospel faith. Or else we have gone this way but later neglected it. This is the case with Simon the Pharisee, who possessed faith as credence but did not practise the faith of the publican. He did not keep it in mind as the background of his own existence. Consequently he became rigid in his judgments and incapable of evaluating the meaning of human situations.

This practical forgetfulness of the spirit of gospel faith can be the cause of so much insensibility, tension and lack of understanding which harm the life of the Church and her communities, because it entrenches itself in a rigidity of judgment deemed necessary as a defence against laxity.

The ford of faith provides us with the right attitude that mediates between the strictness of Simon and the laxity which more or less lets things go and become resigned to mediocrity. It is not true that the only choice we have is between rigidness and leniency. Both positions are wrong – whether it be the leniency that would say: "Let it be, let's try to be human, one cannot demand certain things, times have changed," or the rigidness that would claim: "We must absolutely preserve tradition; woe to us if we give up this or that," an so forth.

Neither too much nor too little permits an authentic consecrated life. Both prevent a realization of true humanness and true femininity and thus deprive society of the message of salvation that the religious life ought to bring to it. The faith that Jesus praises in the sinful woman has been the salvation of her womanhood, her dignity, her humanity, her piety, her truth.

Let us, then, pray to Our Lady, asking her to grant us the faith that she expressed in her human suffering at the foot of the cross and that enabled her not to rebel at the death of her Son but to accept it and experience it in all its reality. Let us ask her to obtain from the Lord the gift of true judgment, at least in its basic expression, for us and for all religious Congregations of men and women, for the clergy, for all the committed movements in the Church and for everyone dedicated to the service of God.

THE SPIRIT OF PETITION AND COMPUNCTION

The mother of Zebedee's sons (Mt 20:20-23)

Let us seek help for our preparatory prayer from a passage of the Prophet Zechariah:

> "And I will pour out on the house of David and the inhabitants of Jerusalem a spirit of compassion and supplication so that, when they look on him whom they have pierced, they shall mourn for him, as one mourns for an only child, and weep bitterly over him as one weeps over a first-born" (Zech 12:10).

In the light of this text let us again read some words of John the Evangelist on the death of Jesus:

> Jesus said, "It is finished"; and he bowed his head and gave up his spirit.
> Since it was the day of Preparation, in order to prevent the bodies from remaining on the cross on the sabbath (for that sabbath was a high day), the Jews asked Pilate that their legs might be broken, and that they might be taken away. So the soldiers came and broke the legs of the first, and of the other who had been crucified with him; but when they came to Jesus, and saw that he was already dead, they did not break his legs. But one of the soldiers pierced his side with a spear; and at once there came out blood and water. He who saw it has borne witness – his testimony is true, and he knows that he tells the truth – that you also may believe as well. For these things took place that the scripture might be fulfilled, *"Not a bone of him*

shall be broken."And again another scripture says: *"They shall look on him whom they have pierced"* (Jn 19:30-37).

"O Mary, witness of all these events, help us to enter into the mystery of the cross. Place in our hearts that spirit of grace and prayer, of petition and compunction which the Lord wants to pour out on his city in the last times. We want to entreat you, using the ancient words: 'Fac me tecum pie flere, crucifixo condolere, donec ego vixero.' Let me weep with you all my life long, in a weeping and a spirit of petition that will never cease and will continually bedew the soul's terrain, loosening the hardened clods of the heart."

This is the grace we are asking: *the permanent spirit of petition and compunction by which the gospel spirit of faith is translated into lived piety.* And we make this request through the intercession of St Charles Borromeo, who is often represented in the act of weeping over the passion.

Since we want to meditate on the spirit of penitent faith, we can ask whether Mary experienced this since she was conceived without sin. Our answer is a definite yes, although she experienced it in a singular manner. In order to understand this, we recall what St Thérèse of the Child Jesus once said of herself:

> "One could think that it is just because I have not sinned that I have such great confidence in the Lord. Do tell them, Mother, that had I committed every possible crime I would have the same confidence. I would think that this multitude of offences were like drops of water cast into a burning brazier" (*Novissima Verba,* July 11).

This is what we mean by the spirit of petition and humility. It is the attitude which permitted the same saint to consider herself "seated at the table of sinners," united with all the sinners among her own people, petitioning and offering herself as a victim for them.

Mary too, in her sinlessness, knew that she was redeemed by the blood of her Son and can, therefore, accompany us on our journey.

The mother of Zebedee's sons

The gospel text which I have selected in order to deepen the spirit of penitent faith presents us with a noteworthy episode often left unconsidered: the request of Zebedee's sons. The passage should be read in connection with that immediately preceding it, in which we find the third announcement of the passion:

> And as Jesus was going up to Jerusalem, he took the twelve disciples aside, and on the way he said to them, "Behold, we are going up to Jerusalem, and the Son of man will be delivered to the chief priests and scribes, and they will condemn him to death, and deliver him to the Gentiles to be mocked and scourged and crucified, and he will be raised on the third day."
> Then the mother of the sons of Zebedee came up to him, with her sons, and kneeling before him she asked him for something. And he said to her, "What do you want?" She said to him, "Command that these two sons of mine may sit, one at your right hand and the other at your left, in your kingdom." But Jesus answered, "You do not know what you are asking. Are you able to drink the cup that I am to drink?" They said to him, "We are

able." He said to them, "You will drink my cup, but to sit at my right hand and at my left is not mine to grant, but it is for those for whom it has been prepared by my Father." And when the ten heard it, they were indignant at the two brothers. But Jesus called them to him and said, "You know that the rulers of the Gentiles lord it over them, and their great men exercise their authority over them. It shall not be so among you; but whoever would be great among you must be your servant, and whoever would be first among you must be your slave; even as the Son of man came not to be served but to serve, and to give his life as a ransom for many" (Mt 20:17-28).

The prediction of the passion which precedes the mother's request, strongly emphasizes the discrepancy of the latter with the attitude of Jesus, who had just spoken of death. And this discrepancy is again placed in relief by the rebellion of the other apostles and the conclusions that Jesus draws. This passage, which applies to everyone in the Church, is particularly valid for those who meditate on their own responsibility towards society – Let us save society! I said that from the beginning! – For you it means the possibility of assuming full responsibility toward humanity. Many indeed are the pitfalls, snares and camouflages of this assumption of responsibility. We can always interpret it as a privilege or a kind of new possibility for taking the lead!

Hence the importance of our reflection on the spirit of petition and compunction. As usual, I shall outline a few aspects of the text as an introduction to your own personal meditation and contemplation.

The mother

At the very beginning of the account the "mother of the sons of Zebedee" is given prominence, and this sounds a bit strange. One could have said: the mother of James and John. Probably this description derives from the fact that they were mentioned from the beginning as "the sons of Zebedee" and are two of the first disciples:

> As he walked by the Sea of Galilee, he saw two brothers, Simon who is called Peter and Andrew his brother, (their father is not mentioned, perhaps because he was already dead, or because he was not a fisherman) casting a net into the sea; for they were fishermen. And he said to them, "Follow me, and I will make you fishers of men." Immediately they left their nets and followed him. And going on from there he saw two other brothers, James the son of Zebedee and John his brother, in the boat with Zebedee their father, mending their nets, and he called them. Immediately, they left the boat and their father, and followed him (Mt 4:18-22).

It is a question, therefore, of a family in which paternal authority was present and it was normal to mention the father, who probably was a patriarch of rather forceful habits and also exercised a psychological influence in the life of his sons.

We notice that the parallel text in Mark does not include the mother in the scene. Scholars have questioned whether Mark abbreviated the account, as I personally hold, or whether Matthew wanted to make the scene clearer by letting the real instigator of the whole affair, the mother, emerge. It is difficult to choose between the two versions. I have selected Matthew because it seems to develop the psychological background of the two brothers better.

For her part, the mother is a person of note in the gospel. Coming from Capernaum and being the mother of James and John, she was surely close to Jesus' family and knew Mary well. That is why Matthew reminds us that she was even present at the foot of the cross. Linked, therefore, to Jesus' destiny, she is one of the women who, supporting him with her own goods, served him on his journeys, often listened to his preaching and shared in the Master's apostolic activity with enthusiasm. In brief, she belongs to the group of the most faithful disciples, and her request is certainly meant in earnest.

We may, then, ask her: "How did it ever occur to you to make this request so officially? (The gesture of prostrating herself clearly indicates the official character of her petition.) It is a request that you have surely reflected upon day and night."

The mother will respond that, basically, she represents that which is still active in us. Like her we too have given everything. Nevertheless there is always present in us the expectation of something that will gratify and recompense us. Perhaps this mother saw none of the expectations that she had placed in her sons being realized and thought: "Things are being reorganized, and my boys are being excluded from it; the others are forming a coalition and are leaving them out of it." It is the instinct, although we do not always voice it, by which we look for and count on a certain result. Something beautiful and great will happen! And when we notice that our hopes are not realized, we conclude that we have blundered and not done what we should have. How many of these anxieties spoil and eat away at our life like a termite just when we least expect it! Sometimes it is well-meaning persons who say to us: "How is it that others are succeeding and you not? Why are you not getting ahead?" Such blows leave us so disconcerted that we begin to believe our friends are right.

All this is worldliness in its most subtle forms making itself manifest within us. Then by contrast, we understand the value of Mary's silence which, after the great lights of the Annunciation and a few glimmers at the birth of Jesus, saw nothing happen any more, for years and even decades. Mary, who kept in her heart the secrets and the words of the "beginning," could have been tempted to expect a minimum of gratification, some event or something impressive. But the only – and for the most part disconcerting – event that occurs to break Mary's silence is the flight of the twelve-year-old Jesus. The more we yield to the illusion of something that ought to happen as a compensation for our sacrifices, the more we admire the heroism of Mary, who does not comment or speak. She accepts, because she is *sure* of Jesus.

The mother of the sons of Zebedee does not possess the same confidence as Mary but expects something. She wants an assurance from Jesus, a word of promise. Nevertheless she does not ask for herself, although she herself has made a personal sacrifice in order to follow the Master. She petitions for her sons who have done so much and have "gambled" themselves completely. Fear that they may be overlooked makes her uneasy. Sometimes we too petition for others, for our friends: they have worked so hard, have served the Church, and we would like to see them receive at least a minimum of recognition, at least a word, a note, or a promotion. But nothing happens.

Let us try to understand the reality of these sentiments that characterize our daily life, our Christian communities and all the organizations: our action in society and in our community is not free from this desire for recognition and gratification.

The sons

Jesus reproves neither the mother nor the sons. He understands them and even teases them a bit: "You do not know what you are asking." But he does not take offence, in contrast to the other apostles, who starting from the same premise as the two brothers, feel themselves in turn passed over.

The sons are James and John.

James will be the first martyr apostle, the first of the Twelve to give his life for the faith. His death is described in chapter 12 of the Acts of the Apostles.

John is the evangelist, the apostle of candour, of purity, of truth, of transparency.

Nevertheless, in our text these very generous brothers, ever ready to dedicate themselves, show themselves susceptible to becoming entangled in the nets of daily life. They have abandoned their nets – and maybe their father called after them, scolding them for it; they have accomplished the heroic gesture of leaving home, but the nets reappear.

Note the psychological shrewdness of placing them in relation to their mother. They consent to her request and, although they grasp the inopportuneness of it, they do not restrain her. Their line of reasoning follows the same outline as that of the mother: "It is by no means for us; it is for her, for our father. They have made such great sacrifices for us and now they ought to have some recompense. They should be able to show our friends and relatives that it was all worthwhile, that their sons have 'arrived' and have a good position."

On the heroic James and the transparent, contemplative John there falls a shadow of subtle small-mindedness. Nothing bad in itself as long as they are not asking anything wrong. They simply want to be near Jesus, and yet they are corrupted by the little worm of worldliness. Even following Jesus and sacrificing themselves with him, their heart has become hardened anew. In fact, here is surfacing the phenomenon of *hardness of heart* so often recorded in the gospels, of the heart that withers almost fatally, of the heart that does not always succeed in being above situations and even when it seems to have become stabilized shrivels up again. Obviously this is not the same hardness of heart as that of the impious who says, "There is no God. Eternal life is a nice fable. Better enjoy ourselves and do as we please!"

It is the hardness of heart of the apostles so frequently reproved by Jesus: "How hard and slow is your heart to believe! You have eyes but do not see; you have ears but do not hear. Do you really not understand?" How often the Master thus addressed the apostles, these great saints whom we venerate as pillars of the Church! They too, like ourselves, were subject to this progressive, recurring aridity of the heart. We get things done, are active, work and dedicate ourselves, but the worldliness that is linked to the element of family, culture and ancestry remains. None of us can completely sever ourselves from our family, environment and mentality. Rather, the older we get the more readily we return to the manner of reasoning and evaluating of our original family group. While we are young we feel detached and dedicate ourselves with energy and enthusiasm. Then little by little as our strength fails, our recollections increase and affections, preoccupations and anxieties regarding this or that relative emerge again.

Often it is difficult to discern, because charity has to be preserved and the material needs of relatives are real. Under these disguised forms of nepotism that reappear with age, however, there is always a certain attempt to recover what has already been given with so much joy. We had hoped for some promotion or other and seeing that it does not come, we at least try to assist our family, our nieces and nephews, and so on! We have to be seriously on our guard against this *hardness of heart* which takes hold of us with increasing years, although we ought not to be surprised, for Jesus heals us patiently.

In our gospel passage, we really have to admire Jesus' patience. He calls the Twelve to him, and by giving himself as an example of one who has come to serve and to give his life, he restores the Twelve to the rhythm of his own heart. That is the very thing we should do: betake ourselves continually to the heart of the Crucified One, together with Mary, in a spirit of petition and compunction, the spirit that animated St Charles. Only in this way is it possible to dissolve the sclerosis of heart and mind that inevitably crops up again in individuals, communities, groups and institutions. No one is exempt from this blight of the heart. Only the spirit of penitent faith and repeated tears keep the clods of our spirit bedewed, as it were, to offset the weight of our habits and traditions, of our ties to family, kinship and friends – not in what is beautiful and constructive about them but in their restraining and limiting aspect.

What Paul wrote to the Galatians we can accept as written to us:

> O foolish Galatians! Who has bewitched you, before whose eyes Jesus Christ was publicly portrayed as crucified? Let me ask you only this: Did you receive the Spirit by works of the law, or by hearing with faith? Are you so foolish? Having begun with the Spirit, are you now ending with the flesh? Did you experience so many things in vain? – if it really is in vain (Gal 3:1-4).

It is interesting to note that the form of hardening of the heart denounced by Paul is likewise a form of mental rigidity. The heart can reclothe itself in zeal for the law and in a rigidness that screens the lack of a penitent spirit. This explains certain situations and facts that arise now and then in the Church. Think, for example, of the resistance against Vatican Council II, think of the movement named after Bishop Lefèbvre, which clothes itself in severity in order to nestle in past traditions and remembrances, in what was handed down and what one now fears to abandon.

This hardness of heart, which even penetrates the stages of the Church's history, explains the oscillation – we referred to this in the meditation on the sinful woman in Simon's house – between an external rigour and a remissness which actually covers up an attitude of heart not fully converted, not fully humble and contrite. Zeal for the law, for orthodoxy and observance can mask a return to one's own human habits, to traditions inasmuch as they provided security and warmth and not because they spurred us on to cast ourselves into God's infinity. Likewise, remissness, indulgence and amiability that appear under the banner of the needs of humanitarianism and psychology can veil the renouncement of that perfection to which we have really committed ourselves.

There is only one remedy for avoiding Paul's reproach to the Galatians: "You were running well; who hindered you from obeying the truth?" (5:7) and that is compunction, passing to penitent gospel faith without which there is no progress in the spiritual life of individuals or communities.

The crisis of development in the spiritual life

The crisis of development in the spiritual life is the principal cause of every other crisis in the religious life. From the phenomenological viewpoint it is the crisis that follows the successes of the time of fervour and does not know how to endure the lengthy periods of silence through which Mary passed. After the first profession when more attention was given to group enthusiasm and organizational dynamics than to the mercy of God, there is a standstill. We notice that we still have so many faults and that self-love is still deeply rooted; we tend to blame it all on the others, on the unhelpful environment and the sluggish community, on the un-updated theology, on lack of culture, on the group's lack of zeal for the aged, the poor, the isolated, and so forth. If on the contrary we do not blame the others, then we become despondent because we are unsuccessful in improving. The retreats, the sermons, general chapters and proposals for renewal have been to no avail. We say to ourselves: "I was too much of a dreamer. I should not have deceived myself. I let myself be misled by reading the lives of the saints (Who knows anyway if they were as they are described!). Perfection is not for me. It is better to be more realistic and contented." We can even go further and say: "Had I known that it would end up like this, that I would not be able to use my abilities and talents, perhaps I would not have made the move. In any case, after what I have experienced I do not feel able today to advise anyone to make the choice I did."

These are signs of this crisis of development in the spiritual life. There are still more dangerous symptoms, such as those in which the attitude of mediocrity is rationalized and transformed into a cult of spontaneity, or on the contrary, of spiritual aggressiveness. Even more dangerous and subtle is the going so far as to deny a bad conscience: "God loves me with my sins. I can very well live with them. The Lord does not need my changing and will save me all the same."

There was a time when such manifestations were called Pelagianism or Lutheranism. It is true that nowadays heresies are not so much in fashion, and a crisis of development in the spiritual life will not always lead us to heretical conclusions. Nevertheless it certainly leads to a basically common outcome: in every one of these forms of aberration, prayer is no longer taken seriously. Either it becomes a matter of perfect execution of some practices, or something vague and nebulous that is expressed as follows: "It is useless to go to church.

I find the Lord in nature and in my fellow men and women. Therefore I am always at prayer."

What is the solution? It is to accept God's mysterious, long silence with humility, trust and petition; to pass through the Sea of Reeds, ceasing to circumvent it in search of other ways or ways out; *to be sure of Jesus,* our merciful Head and Liberator, who loves us in order to make us better and not to leave us as we are.

Jesus is not alarmed if after so many years we are still at the same point. He does, however, want us to be ready to begin anew today as though it were the first day, as though I had only today received the angel's message. And this *certainty in Jesus* expresses itself in compunction which continually renews the miracle of baptism. God's mercy pardons seventy times seven and is not astonished at the mother of Zebedee's sons nor at Peter and his denial. But it is mercy that does not make any truce with our faults and sins. This is the middle way, the solution of Catholic asceticism or spirituality, which believes in the power of pardon and in the renewing power of grace. The spiritual life, then, is dynamic and is made holy in this dynamism. After thirty years it seems to us that we still have the same faults as in the beginning. In reality the person has changed, has been transformed by faith, love, humility and daily penance, even though the temperament still leaves something to be desired in some of its outward expressions.

In other words, the way of penance – and of the sacrament of penance – preserves us from all the attitudes we make use of in order to camouflage ourselves and it impels us through the Spirit toward the perfect and total offering of ourselves to the Father in Christ.

It is true that the sacrament of penance can be misused – and this is often why we abandon it – but the resolute desire to use it, despite God's silence, is a sure preservation against hardness of heart. It revitalizes that New Testament virtue of vigilance which is the hallmark of those who never give up or lose their way or become discouraged.

May Mary help us to enter into her humble and ever vigilant silence, to lead our life of penance as an immersion in the merciful blood of Jesus crucified, who is our justification.

THE MEETING OF
MARY AND ELIZABETH

Homily
1st Reading: Is 9:2-4.6-7; 2nd Reading: Lk 1:39-47

Mary's Queenship, which the Church celebrates liturgically on this feast, is wholly related to the Kingship of Jesus. Everything that Mary possesses and signifies is related to Christ and, in fact, the words of the first reading call to mind those of the angel at the Annunciation as they draw our attention to the fact that "for to us a child is born..." whose dominion will extend "upon the throne of David, and over his kingdom".

Mary as Queen represents woman arrived at the pinnacle of fulfillment, the summit of the mission of every woman in society and in history. In considering her as Queen, we can understand how woman is called to complete the same journey. It is, therefore, important to gather a few of the aspects of Mary's Queenship as they are indicated in the liturgical texts.

1. *The first reading* speaks of joy and exultation: "Thou hast multiplied the nation, thou hast increased its joy." It is this increase of joy and exultation that renders human life and history worth living. Joy and exultation occur in exceptional circumstances: once annually at harvest time and once every few years when the spoils of victory are divided.

In these cases even man – ordinarily trained to

keep himself within restricted limits of demonstrativeness – rejoices and exults for joy. This is seen in the dance of the reapers over the abundant harvest or the song of the soldiers over the distribution of the booty.

The Queenship of Mary consists in imbuing the human with that needed "extra" which is the exuberance of joy, of communication, of contentment, of the breath of nature and of the heart. Queenship is equivalent to placing the crown on necessity and duty: without this crown things remain pallid, uncertain, flat, colourless and unattractive.

This indispensable "extra" manifests itself above all in the area of human communication where the typical presence or absence of humanness is more easily detected. And I am thinking of how much inability to communicate there is in society nowadays and how much frustration all this causes! I am thinking of families – and there are many – in which there is no real friendship, cordial exchange or communicative attitude.

On the other hand to reveal oneself to another truly is difficult because it requires discretion and respect for the mystery of the other. In the 60's and 70's through the influence of psychology from across the Atlantic there was a gust of communication in the form of writings, research projects and experiments. This included various kinds of therapy and techniques, sometimes useful since they were based on the study of worthwhile psychology. I myself recall having participated in some of these group sessions in communication and having derived a certain benefit from them. Being obliged to live for twelve days with a group of people from morning till night certainly does release the mechanism of "group communication" and makes one acquainted with "group dynamics".

Nevertheless there was a basic misunderstanding, perhaps unarticulated, in all that frenzy over psychological and therapeutic communication, namely, that the person is fundamentally incommunicable because he is unique and unrepeatable and carries within him a mystery of incommunicability that may not be forced but only accepted in love.

2. *The second reading* shows us Mary as Queen of communication and receptiveness.

Indeed, the mystery of the Visitation is the mystery of mutual communication between two women diverse in age, environment and characteristics, and their reciprocal respectful receptivity. Two women, each of whom bears a secret difficult to communicate, the most intimate and most profound secret that a woman can experience on the plane of natural life – the expectation of a child.

It is difficult for Elizabeth to talk about it on account of her age and the novelty and the strangeness of it. It is difficult for Mary because she cannot divulge the angel's words to anyone. If, according to the gospel narrative, Elizabeth had lived in seclusion for some months in a kind of solitude, Mary's solitude is infinitely greater. This is probably one of the reasons why Mary sets out "with haste". She needs to see someone who understands, and from what the angel has said, she senses that Elizabeth is the most suitable person. She leaves in haste in order to seek help and not only because she wants to help her cousin. It is beautiful to think of Mary's willingness to let herself be helped.

When the two women meet, Mary is Queen in greeting the other first; she is Queen in knowing how to pay honour to the other, for her Queenship is one of courteous attentiveness, as ought to be the case for every woman. And her attention produces an extraordinary effect: "When Elizabeth heard the greeting of Mary, the babe leaped in her womb." Elizabeth feels understood to her depths, and what was previously a cause for fear on her part is transformed into joy. She understands herself as joy, as exultation in her son. At the same time, however, she comprehends the mystery that Mary has not yet expressed to her: "Blessed are you among women, and blessed is the fruit of your womb!" It would have been logical for her to say: "I am filled with joy." Instead of speaking of herself, with the intensity with which she speaks of herself she tells Mary who she is: the most blessed of all women.

We can readily imagine Mary's exultation and astonishment when, without having said a word, she feels herself understood, accepted, recognized, loved and exalted.

"Why is this granted to me that the mother of my Lord should come to me?" Elizabeth knows everything, she has understood everything. Has she, then, had a revelation? Not at all. She has simply let herself become involved in Mary's greeting and thanks to this greeting she has understood Mary and accepted her in fullness of joy: "Blessed is she who believed that the promise made her by the Lord would be fulfilled."

Mary feels herself praised for something that was most specifically hers: she had entrusted herself to the Word, she had invested her entire self in her "fiat" and had summed up her whole life in it. She had crossed the ford of faith, abandoning herself completely to this new mode of existence and life. Her faith, inexplicable to others, now finds recognition.

The mystery of the Visitation, therefore, speaks to us of an interpenetration of souls, of a most discreet mutual acceptance that does not wear itself out with multiplying words and does not require a flood of elocution. Rather, with simple glints of light, with torches in the night, it permits a communication and a recognition that is perfect.

These are the queenly attitudes that Mary inserts into history and humanity, above all through those who closely follow her in consecrating their life to faith in the Word. To you Mary gives the grace of being queens, of expressing this kind and this manner of salvation in history.

"O Mary, grant us to know you, to understand you and to accept your way of leading and saving! Help us to be queens of communication in the Church, of that attentive, discreet, sincere, authentic communication which is perhaps the most vital desire of the hearts of today's men and women. You know that in opposition to this desire gigantic obstacles seem to arise like castles of smoke that impede communication on the level of truth and humanness. Help us and our communities to be as you are, to be as you would have us be."

CONTEMPLATION

Martha and Mary (Lk 10:38-42)

"Mary, Mother of Jesus and our Mother, we place ourselves with you at the foot of your Son's cross, asking you to help us enter into the mystery of his life and death; to dwell in his Heart; to remain at his feet in an attitude of listening and contemplation. Arouse in us, Mary, your sentiments of participation in the suffering of Christ and of the world.

You see how imperfect our words are and how far removed our concepts are from the truth that you live. Help each one of us; help everyone who is united with our prayer and our adoration. Grant us joy in your Son by the Holy Spirit's grace, which we implore from the power of the Father. Amen."

Martha and Mary

The gospel passage on which we shall now meditate is well known and is reported for us by the evangelist Luke:

> Now as they went on their (Jesus with the Apostles) way, he entered a village; and a woman named Martha received him into her house. And she had a sister called Mary, who sat at the Lord's feet and listened to his teaching. But Martha was distracted with much serving; and she went to him and said, "Lord, do you not care that my sister has left me to serve alone? Tell her then to help me." But the Lord answered her, "Martha, Martha, you are

anxious and troubled about many things; one thing is needful. Mary has chosen the good portion, which shall not be taken away from her" (Lk 10:38-42).

This text is so rich in psychological, human, religious and theological elements that we could almost spend an entire retreat just reflecting on the attitudes it contains. I limit myself to proposing to you a meditation on the following points: Who is Martha? Who is Mary? Who are we?

Martha

Evidently Martha is the lady of the house, for it is she who is mentioned as the woman to whose house Jesus goes with his disciples. She is, therefore, responsible for the entire housekeeping. Likewise on reading the episode of the raising of Lazarus in John's gospel (11:1-43), we are given the impression that Martha is the elder sister.

On this account alone, Martha's reasons are valid. As the lady of the house she has to honour the guest and do everything so that nothing will be lacking to him. Then, too, the guest is not alone and, therefore, it is clear that her preoccupation mounts. The atmosphere is somewhat marked by agitation and anxiety in the desire to have everything go as well as possible without any lack of the customary forms of attention. So Martha wants to succeed in giving a truly worthy hospitality, and her fear of not doing so does not at all surprise us.

Behind this backdrop, which is normal, we notice that Martha is in reality cultivating what we might call the masculine ideal of efficiency, applied to housekeeping but nevertheless an ideal of success. It *has* to succeed; things *have* to be carried out exactly as they should be. Then at a certain point it happens that the ideal of efficiency so rigidly cultivated makes her lose sight of the essence of the situation, the view of the whole. In her anxiety to show herself above the situation she totally loses its sense. In fact, we see that a ludicrous reversal of roles takes place: she wants to honour Jesus as guest and ends up by reproaching him!

Martha had at heart the very beautiful ideal of Hebrew patriarchal hospitality (for the Hebrew, the guest is king and lord and is given the place of honour). Endeavouring at all costs to achieve this ideal, she finishes by putting herself in place of the guest and commanding him as though he were her subordinate: *"Tell her then to help me."* This is the mess which Martha has got into with her reasonable and rigorous desire for efficiency: she has distorted the meaning of things and failed to understand anything about Jesus. To her mind now, everything is going as though Jesus had come only for a good meal, whereas Jesus is honoured by being acknowledged as Master. This did not require a long period of spiritual decline. In the course of two to three hours she has lost sight of the truth, and the ideal of success has deprived her of that overview, the capacity for synthesis, which permitted Our Lady to see through to the point of the situation during the banquet in Cana.

With great psychological finesse, Luke says that she was distracted with all the serving. So the meaning of what was taking place escaped her.

Mary

Mary is the younger sister, and it would be logical for her to help. In this sense Martha is right. The younger sister should cooperate and leave Jesus and the apostles in peace.

But what does Mary do? She "sat at the Lord's feet and listened to his teaching". Here it is important to note every aspect of the description.

"At the Lord's feet" means that she honours him as Master, showing that she has perfectly grasped Jesus' intention: he comes as Master, and she receives him as such.

She *"listened to his teaching"*: Jesus' deepest desire is to give, to communicate the Word. Mary fully realizes the gospel Beatitude: "Blessed are they who hear the Word of God and put it into practice." She has understood the point of the situation, what matters, and has caught it with the gift of synthesis like Mary in Cana.

I believe it is not without reason that, in the mystery of Holy Scripture, this woman's name is Mary, and she is listening. She is a symbol of Mary, Mother of Jesus and silent listener of the Word.

Here the silent mystery of Mary of Nazareth becomes transparent to us. There is practically no account of what she did during Jesus' life and even less of her activity in the early Church. The Mother of Jesus remains among us as *the listening woman,* image of listening humanity and the listening Church; image of the basic attitude of man, who in his radical openness to the supernatural is defined as "hearer of the Word". Here is delineated the very mystery of humanity which is fully itself when it is at Jesus' feet listening to his Word. Naturally, this ability to listen in silence does not negate other realities, which, however, derive their meaning from this one.

Hence Mary of Bethany is a figure of Mary of Nazareth and at the same time of the vocation of the woman religious, which includes the ability to listen silently to the Word, so that humanity may come to comprehend the breadth of its own vocation and assume a listening attitude towards God.

Each one of us ought to see ourselves reflected in Mary and compare the value that she gives to activity with the value that she gives to listening, not in order to play one off against the other but to coordinate them, in keeping with one's own real vocation, in such a way that listening always has priority.

From meditation to contemplation

For our life I would like to underline two important aspects of this episode. First of all, there is the passage from meditation to contemplation, and we can return to Jesus' reproach: "Martha, Martha, you are anxious and troubled about many things, one thing is needful."

Notice how affectionately Jesus speaks. He mentions her name twice in a double personal appeal. It is not a real and proper rebuke but a revelation meant to open her eyes. This woman is being set before a mirror: "What are you doing? You are preoccupied and upset by many things!" She is simply presented with the situation without a word of bias or comment. And Jesus' manner of expression is full of evangelical, pastoral and mystical meaning.

Here we can see two ways of serving Jesus represented. One can be called *service of the Kingdom;* it is a good and necessary way. All the baptized are called to commit and dedicate themselves totally to the cause of God's Kingdom. Religious consecration, then, binds in a particular manner to this service, which necessarily admits of a variety of practical activities, good in themselves, as long as they remain within the framework of service to the Kingdom. There is a need to teach, housework, cook, study, tend the sick, assist the youth, give instruction in prayer, listen to confidences, and so forth.

Nevertheless, beginning with and in all these occupations there is a second way, in which all attain unity, namely, that of *service to the King,* to the person of Jesus. Progress in the spiritual life is measured by the ever increasing ability to unify the multiple acivities within adoration and loving service to the one Person. While it is true that from the very beginning we follow and love Jesus, in reality the psychological tone of daily life is necessarily determined by the multiplicity of activities. And it is not without exertion, not without spiritual discipline and not without a special grace that we attain that integration in which the most important thing is to serve, adore, love, praise and listen to the Lord above all. This second level is the one that counts, gives meaning to the rest, and produces and arouses attitudes of serenity, peace and joy, which are fruits of the Holy Spirit.

Now both levels take shape in the spiritual exercise proper, that is, prayer, which is called meditation and contemplation.

– *Meditation* is the exercise which, beginning with prayerful reading of Scripture, reflects on the various values presented in the text. It bears, therefore, the character of multiplicity of subject matter, thoughts, reflections and propositions. It is absolutely necessary to practise this. It is also a great grace of God, for by the power of the Holy Spirit it arouses in those who practise it dispositions of charity, truth, justice, chastity, forgiveness, mercy, joy, patience, long-suffering and foresight.

To attain a mature spiritual personality, meditation is indispensable and, therefore, fundamental in the religious life and in early formation. But if we were to regard meditation as an end in itself, we would run the risk of being like Martha, of losing ourselves and forgetting the sense of unity.

– It is *contemplation* that unifies the various meditative exercises. It consists in looking at the Lord, Jesus, the centre and synthesis of all God's words. In looking at him, we are satisfied with him beyond any thoughts; we nourish ourselves in his Person, let ourselves be attracted by him and in him see the Father's face.

Contemplation is a pure gift of God, and it is clear that we cannot force it in ourselves. If we pretend to arrive at it by our own devices and without having prepared the way by the work of meditation, we commit a mistake. It is necessary to go the way of humility that begins with reading the sacred text and passes through meditation, which in turn gradually becomes more simple and open us to the gift of the Spirit. At a certain point we shall arrive at that spiritual moment in which our glance becomes concentrated on the Crucified in contemplation, adoration and listening.

No one may presume to be at any certain point of the way, and with the help of a spiritual director, each one ought to recognize when his moment has come. God, of course, retains the sovereign freedom to introduce a soul to contemplation by letting it bypass the ordinary stages.

When we read in the life of Thérèse of the Child Jesus of the difficulty she had meditating and following the spiritual exercises and of the dryness she found in them, we realize that from the very beginning she was granted a prayer of simple contemplation.

But I repeat that it would be dangerous to want to reach contemplation by omitting Scripture reading and meditation. Above all in an apostolic vocation it is very important to nourish oneself abundantly on the many "words of God," so that when the Lord wills it we shall be able to contemplate in truth and humility the Word present in and behind all the "words of God".

The attitudes of Martha and Mary are, therefore, not opposed to one another but complement one another and are related. Martha's services permit Mary to listen, and Mary's listening gives meaning to Martha's service.

Gospel virginity

The second meaning of this episode which I wish to emphasize for our life is suggested by a remark that is very difficult to translate.

Martha "was distracted with much serving"; in Greek *e de Marta periespàto perì pollèn diakonìan.* The verb *peri-espàto* means to strain oneself, to have spasms. This, then, is a spasmodic kind of tension experienced by a person who is under the influence of a thousand occupations and in the desire to succeed at all costs, holds her breath in order to arrive at the goal.

This is the only place in the New Testament in which this word occurs. There is, however, a passage in which its opposite appears: "aperispàstos" – without tension or spasm and, therefore, peacefully. The text is in Paul's First Letter to the Corinthians:

> I say this for your own benefit not to lay any restraint upon you, but to promote good order and secure your undivided devotion to the Lord (1 Cor 7:35).

The word translated by "undivided devotion", meaning "without distraction" is in Greek *aperispàstos,* without anxiety. It indicates the unity of our life peacefully directed to the Lord Jesus. That is what St Paul describes as the psychological reality of virginity: the whole of life oriented to the person of Christ.

Accordingly, by Christian virginity, whose inner mystery surfaces in the figure of Mary of Bethany, is meant total dedication to the Lord, remaining at his feet. The Apostle likewise says in the First Letter to the Corinthians:

> I mean, brethren, the appointed time has grown very short; from now on, let those who have wives live as though they had none; and those who mourn as though they were not mourning; and those who rejoice as though they were not rejoicing, and those who buy as though they had no goods, and those who deal with the world as though they had no dealings with it. For the form of this world is passing away. I want you to be free from anxieties. The unmarried man is anxious about the affairs of the Lord, how to please the Lord... (7:29-32).

Christian virginity is not merely celibacy, a renouncement of marriage. If it were, we could define it as "not belonging to anyone" so as to be at the service of all. Rather, it is a *espousal virginity,* a "belonging to the Lord".

Here a not so facile problem surfaces. Does it make sense to speak of espousals in relation to virginity, or is it not a designation that leads us to anthropological or sociological complications from which it is difficult to extricate ourselves? I believe that we may never use words at random for these definitions and that their precise meaning must be clarified. What does "espousal" mean? Not wanting to define it simply in relation to sensuality and corporality but rather in relation to the person, we can say that *espousal consists in defining oneself in relation to a person;* it is awareness of self in relation to someone. Defined in this way, it profoundly interpellates the mystery of the person and even suggests the mystery of the Holy Trinity. Indeed the Father is he who is related to the Son; the Son is he who is related to the Father; the Spirit is he who is related to the Father and the Son.

This mystery of total giving as in marriage can become an intimate part of the mystery of the person, determining it and constituting its horizon of life. So Christian virginity is understanding oneself not as existing only in and for oneself but in relation to Christ, in virtue of a mutual free act. In this way Christian virginity enters into the intimate sphere of a person's life and envelops it.

Moreover, all this refers to a historico-biblical reality: Jesus freely willed to be defined in relation to a people and willed that a people – by grace, by choice and by love – be defined in relation to his God. *It is the mystery of the Covenant whose basic formula is: "I am your God; you are my people."* It is like saying: I am yours and you are mine. Not infrequently, in fact, the Covenant is expressed in Scripture in nuptial symbols. Think of the Song of Songs, of the book of the Prophet Hosea, of Jesus' parables of the Kingdom that involve a wedding.

It is not easy to "say" these things. With words we scarcely graze them, in the twofold sense that we merely touch the surface and risk pulling off the petals and extracting the perfume. It is contemplation as a gift of God that permits us to intuit the mystery of espousal that characterizes consecrated virginity. It then also becomes a source of interior discipline, of austerity in thought, deed, word and gesture, a form of life and a hallmark of the historical person. The spousal Spirit, who entered Mary's heart and body to generate the Son, teaches us all this. He is the Spirit who, entering into the mystery of our person, leads us to live in the fullness and fruitfulness of the divine Covenant in which Christ is spiritually generated in hearts and in history.

THE GIFT OF GOD

Homily
1st Reading: Ez 36:2-28; 2nd Reading: Mt 22: 1-14

The passage from the Prophet Ezekiel which we have chosen is one of the oldest in the Old Testament and breathes of the Holy Spirit. It is part of that great oracle called the "oracle about the mountains of Israel". In fact, it begins with the words: "Prophesy to the mountains of Israel. Say, 'Mountains of Israel, hear the word of Yahweh.'"

This text of today's liturgy exhibits a grammatical characteristic that can be gathered by simply listening. All its verbs are in the first person. I am going to display... I shall take... and gather... and bring...; I shall pour... I shall cleanse... I shall give... and put...; I shall remove... and give...; I shall put and make you keep... and practise...

Only at the conclusion are the verbs not in the first person. It is the formula of the Covenant, the formula of mutual espousal: "You shall be my people and I will be your God."

The espousal formula does not originate, then, from a human idea or initiative. It is the fruit and terminus of a prolonged divine initiative in which God alone acts in the first person. He acts in favour of his people by virtue of his own power; he acts in the inmost recesses of hearts, reforming the person and society from within; he acts within the sphere of his universal vision of history, of the laws that govern the development of a people, and he acts by placing these laws in the heart. The fundamental truth of biblical revelation is that God acts, does, works.

Looking at it from our point of view, we could express it as follows. We have spoken of so many aspects of consecrated life. Nevertheless, our spiritual experience tells us that we never live up to it. We do not cross the ford of faith; we do not achieve penitent, suppliant gospel faith; we do not succeed in passing from meditation to contemplation; we continue to be preoccupied with a thousand services and not with the King. Often despite our efforts we are left with the impression that we have returned to the starting point and are still on the other side of the Sea of Reeds.

The ford of faith, however, or the passage from the Kingdom to the King, springs from the humble conviction that it is God who acts; the conviction that although from the beginning we have had the viewpoint of theological faith (God created heaven and earth; he is the Maker of all), it has not yet become an inner fountain of spiritual life. It will become such – after so much effort and exertion, after having hit our heads so many times – the moment we recognize that service to the King is a *gift*, contemplation is a *gift*, virginal adhesion of heart to Jesus is a *gift*, the ford of faith is a *gift*.

In this sense the passage from the Prophet Ezekiel is basic. It confronts us with the crucial problem of all Christian and gospel spiritual asceticism. God is always first; his primacy is absolute and unassailable. Our own "doing and acting" is necessary, but in the measure in which we are convinced that it is God who is at work. Even our doing and acting is his gift, and *it is also his gift to comprehend all this*.

We are created to praise his glory and his

unbounded mercy, for it is he who saves us, who loves us first and calls us to bridal union in making us understand the mysterious meaning of his words. He led the saints along the path of dedication, sacrifice and virginity. He alone is great; him alone are we to extol.

We are like the couple in Cana who without knowing it were the object of a maternal solicitude and the power of Christ, the effect of which they were unaware. This discovery is sheer gift and opens the way to awareness of the freedom of the life of faith. We are objects of a maternal solicitude and an efficacious action of Christ the extent of which we are ignorant. It makes us, however, as it did the spouses in Cana, signs of a salvation that embraces the universe.

The ability to contemplate this truth lets us enter the domain of those matters with which we are continually preoccupied, so that we can balance them and order them to the truth of our existence. Our life will not thereby be changed, but our way of looking at it will be. Once our eyes have been opened, we will understand what love we are the object of and what a call has been entrusted to us.

"Grant us, Mary, to recognize what love we are the object of in the mystery of the Eucharist – which is God's gift brought to our very lips and body! Help us to realize that the spiritual life is simple. We are the ones who complicate it as we pursue an ideal of perfection in a corporeal reality that demands continual balancing.

Human life is complicated, like the ascent up a rocky cliff in which it is all a matter of a subtle balance between various movements. But as soon as the rhythms have been learned, the climb fills us with joy. With joy, not with recklessness, because we know that the least blunder can plunge us down into the ravine! *Human life is a simple complication,* in which things become simpler when we regard our entire personal existence as a gift. Then God remains the only One adored, contemplated, loved and served; all the rest is a question of maintaining balance during the ascent. And the joy of working at it helps us to keep looking toward the heights and to strive for the one thing necessary.

Help us, Mary, to simplify our life in the bridal embrace of the one Lord, who accepts us completely, assimilating every instant of our existence into an indescribable harmony, which is the harmony of the Kingdom.

Free us from the danger of believing that we can simplify our life by placing our trust in some particular insignificant practice or in some idea that comes to our mind.

Grant that in the Eucharist we may enjoy a foretaste of that embrace and that Kingdom where God will be all in all. And make us also able to give thanks for this. Amen."

THE SPIRIT OF SACRIFICE AND CONSECRATION

The Lord's servant (Lk 1:26-38)

As we begin our reflection on the gospel passage of the Annunciation, the first sentiment I experience is the desire to remain silent. In fact, I am afraid to speak, as Moses was afraid to look at the burning bush.

At first he approached with a kind of curiosity – as a Father of the Church writes: *"curiosius desideras introire"*. But then he covered his face with his garment for fear of seeing God.

I feel the same way now, for the Annunciation is like a burning bush; it is a mystery that contains everything.

"Mary, speak to us, because we do not know how to speak about you; speak to us, then, yourself. We sense that the mystery of the Annunciation is related to that of the cross. One reflects the other; one is rooted in the other. At the foot of the cross you experienced your Son's death and the Father's infinite love for mankind. Make us comprehend the mysterious roots of this love and penetrate into your 'Yes' to the will of the Father, from whom all originates, in whom all recurs and towhom all returns."

The Lord's servant

Since it would be beyond our scope here to meditate on the entire text of the Annunciation, I propose to consider merely the conclusion:

> Mary said, "I am the handmaid of the Lord; let it be to me according to your word" (Lk 1:38).

These words undoubtedly express an awareness of relationship. Anyone who defines himself as a servant defines his relationship to another person.

At first sight this appears a problem since it really seems to suggest a servile relationship. In fact, the exact word used is *"slave"* – in Greek, *"dûle"*. But if we reflect on the spiritual and biblical context from which it emerges, we understand that it indicates something much more tender and at the same time profound.

Mary's words are the response to the expression that we read in Isaiah:

> Behold my servant, whom I uphold,
> my chosen, in whom my soul delights (Is 42:1).

Mary had surely been nourished by reading the Prophet Isaiah, and this verse resounds in every fibre of her words. There is consonance with the first line – "You see before you the Lord's servant" – and consonance with the second, in the pronouncement of the angel – "You have found favour with God" (Lk 1:30).

Mary identifies herself in relation to God because he has decided to enter into a relationship of choice, contentment and support with her.

Another beautiful consonance is: "I have put my Spirit upon him" (Is 42:1b); and the angel to Mary: "The Holy Spirit will come upon you" (Lk 1:35).

Therefore, in her answer, "I am the handmaid of the Lord," Mary understands herself within the framework of the grace and mission in which the figure of the Servant of Yahweh were situated. Here awareness is that of the mysterious Servant, loved by God and predestined by him to be filled with his Spirit.

Missionary awareness

This awareness is not merely that of the individual but also of the entire people. Mary, who expresses the best in her people, speaks in its name. And we find this reflected in the Isaian meditation:

> But you, Israel, my servant,
>   Jacob, whom I have chosen,
>   the offspring of Abraham, my friend;
> you whom I took from the ends of the earth,
>   and called from its farthest corners,
> saying to you, "You are my servant,
>   I have chosen you and not cast you off;"
> fear not, I am with you,
>   be not dismayed, for I am your God;
> I will strengthen you, I will help you,
>   I will uphold you with my victorious right
>   hand" (Is 41:8-10).

"The Lord is with you," says the angel to Mary, "Do not be afraid, Mary" (Lk 1:28.30).

Mary experiences her awareness in union with that of the people that feels loved, that knows itself to be chosen, that feels God supporting it.

In Isaiah there is still another text expressing this awareness of the people:

> For I am Yahweh, your God,
>   the Holy One of Israel, your Saviour...

Do not be afraid, for I have redeemed you;
I call you by your name...
I surname you, though you do not know me
(Is 45:3.1.4).

In Mary's soul there is a dedication to God that
is hers and is that of the whole of the people of
Israel. Mary is the soul, the voice, the expression of
her people's vocation. So she answers the Lord as
an individual person and as the virgin of Israel, the
daughter of Sion.

Finally behind the awareness of a people, there
is that of humanity, of being a people for a human
race:

"I am the Lord, I have called you in
righteousness,
I have taken you by the hand and kept you;
I have given you as a covenant to the people,
a light to the nations,
to open the eyes that are blind,
to bring out the prisoners from the dungeon,
from the prison those who sit in darkness"
(Is 42:6-7).

The righteous one, my servant, make many...
Therefore I will divide him a portion with the
great (Is 53:11-12).

Mary lives on the wave of the biblical revelation
that is fulfilled in her by the angel's words. She lives
in the threefold awareness of her personal
relationship of dedication to God, of the chorus of
voices of a people, and of responsibility toward all
that is human.

Here we can pause and ask ourselves:

– *How do I conceive my life?* Am I conscious of

this relationship of dependence which definitely modifies human choice? Human choice is, in fact, either one of proper dependence on God or of non-dependence, non-service and non-submission. In the latter case life is distorted and counterfeited by malicious imitations of good that pervert the heart, the spirit and society.

– *Am I aware of belonging to a people?* First of all to the people of Mary and Jesus, for we cannot detach our identity from that of the Hebrew people. Since every Christian has roots in Abraham (in Eucharistic Prayer I of the Mass we say, "Abraham, our Father") there is a bond with the chosen people, the people called to salvation, which is the people of Mary and Jesus. The Church constantly renews her own self-understanding by reflecting on her ties with this people. Of course, these ties are marked by sad historical events and crises, but precisely on this account they ought to be the object of our attention, vigilance and affection.

– Finally, *what is my awareness of peoples?* The right term for it is *missionary awareness.* Even though I have not used the word "missionary" in our meditations, it is evident that what we have said has a missionary flavour. The expression, "Woman among her people," denotes openness to all the rest of humanity, seen in the light of Christ. We know well that all the Church's activity is missionary in character, although it finds its historical and geographical expression defined and emphasized in the foreign missions. Nowadays we no longer distinguish – as we did in the thirties – between a resident and a missionary Church. The entire Church proclaims salvation to the peoples, and as a result missionary activity is all the more an integral part of the nature, culture and very dynamics of the Church's life. This requires attention both on the part of missionary action proper and all other pastoral action, so that they may attain unity.

Christian sacrifice

Now let us reflect on the wish that is more than a Yes, for it expresses joyous, loving acceptance: *"Let it be to me according to your word."* The verb is in the optative mood, expressing a desire, and therefore a Yes with all one's heart.

We are reminded of St Paul's exposition on the spirit of faith in the first eleven chapters of the Letter to the Romans. In other words he talks about what we have described as the spirit of gospel faith of the sinner who has been rehabilitated and justified by God's love. Paul concludes his lengthy exposition by speaking in chapters 12-15 of the *spirit of Christian sacrifice* generated by the spirit of penitent gospel faith:

> I appeal to you, therefore, brethren, by the mercies of God, to present your bodies as a living sacrifice, holy and acceptable to God; which is your spiritual worship (Rom 12:1).

Just as the Apostle summed up the interior life of the Christian – his practice of prayer, penance and intercession – under the spirit of faith, so now he sums up the whole of Christian morality under the spirit of sacrifice. In fact, he continues:

> Do not be conformed to this world, but be transformed by the renewal of your mind, that you may prove what is the will of God, what is good and acceptable and perfect (v. 2).

These two verses introduce us to the practice of discerning what Christian sacrifice is.

Accordingly, after having spoken of the spirit of gospel faith I deem it useful to reflect on the spirit of sacrifice, which is so marvellously evident in Mary's "Yes".

St Augustine, disciple and profound student of St Paul, defines Christian sacrifice as *any act performed in order to enter into a filial communication of love with God*. Sacrifice, then, is a passover, an entry into a divine land.

From the Augustinian viewpoint – shared by all the Fathers – it is not the deed that counts but the purpose of the deed. Consequently, sacrifice too is a grace of the Holy Spirit that arouses the spirit of sacrifice in the redeemed person on the basis of the spirit of faith.

In other words, we can say that sacrifice understood in an objective sense is the person himself who, prompted by love, passes from attention to a multiplicity of things to the one dedication of his personal existence to God. This makes of the person's life an act of love, and this is sacrifice beyond compare.

Moreover, in order to call it Christian we must bring this reflection to its proper end, namely, the fundamental, principal sacrifice, that of Calvary, in which Christ offers himself in order to bring the entire Church, his spouse, to the Father's glory in the resurrection.

In the Eucharist, the Sacrifice of the Altar is related to that of Calvary and brings those who participate in it with love into Jesus' Pasch.

So our entire life as a Christian sacrifice is related to the Eucharist, which in turn is related to the cross, the perfect sacrifice, the total dedication of the man Christ to the Father's will and love, and is able to draw all humanity to itself.

Fundamental option

How does sacrifice enter into our daily life? By the "right direction of heart," formerly called the good intention. This is a summary of Christian asceticism. The person who has invested his entire existence in the resolve to want to please God alone enters into Christ's sacrifice and thereby into the Father's Kingdom. He shares in God's fullness and makes the realities that he sanctifies by the right direction of heart share in it too.

After Christ's sacrifice, Mary's "Yes" is clearly the image, beginning, consequence and summit of all human and Christian perfection. Mary's "Yes" comprises the orientation of her entire life to God and accepts in advance all Christ's choices from Bethlehem to the cross. That is why I said at the beginning of this meditation that the scene of the cross is already contained in the Annunciation. The right direction of heart in its essential degree has another name: *fundamental option*. It is an option, however, which should be understood in a dynamic sense, for it is not sufficient to have made it only once. Rather, it is a vital tendency of love toward the good pleasure of God the Father, towards what pleases him, and it is a disposition that informs the whole life.

This option, renewed in prayer and above all at holy Mass, is like a living flame that imparts vigour and form to all moral choices, making them Christian choices.

It is important to live morality as a dynamism, a tending toward the good, toward the better, a total dedication to the divine design in which man finds the fullness of sonship and true self-realization. The absence or neglect of a dynamic concept of morality inevitably leads to shallowness and to scruples; it leads to all those forms of moralism that can be reduced to asking whether a thing is more or less allowed and how far one may go. All this certainly has some logical value and yet it has a depressing effect and is scarcely authentic for human life which as such is intensity, gift, vigour and largesse. It can lead to sullenness, sadness, indolence and discussions. In the community or group there arise quarrels over privileges, shirking of difficulties and sheer legalism.

Without the dynamic aspect of the fundamental option the view of the whole is lost, as well as the true significance of human existence, which is living water continuously poured out in abundance from above and not stagnant water.

I believe that in many cases – for example, where either the faithful or their pastors stay away from the confessional – this can be explained by shallowness of moral dynamism. In truth, the sacrament of penance is meaningful and valuable in the measure in which it makes a person progress from bad to good and from good to better. All these reflections are suggested by Mary's "Yes".

The person who is intent on this "Yes" is always seeking what pleases God in everything; in other words, he practises discernment.

In the Letter to the Romans, discernment comes immediately after sacrifice: "to present your bodies as a living sacrifice... which is your spiritual worship" (Rom 12:1).

Discernment is quite different from the meticulous punctiliousness of the person who lives in legalistic shallowness or with the pretence of perfectionism. It is an impulse of love that knows how to distinguish between good and better, between what is helpful in itself and helpful now, between what generally works and what on the other hand needs to be fostered now. Discernment is fundamental to apostolic activity, in which it is necessary to choose the better and not to content oneself with doing good, with saying a good word or being a good person. Lack of will to discern the better often renders pastoral ministry monotonous and repetitive. Pious deeds are multiplied and traditional ceremonies repeated without correctly perceiving their meaning, but for the sake of complying with custom and making oneself irreprehensible before God.

Today's young people have a keen sense of dynamic search and should be formed in savouring the better and not merely the good. The fundamental option towards the perfect realization of intimacy with the Father in the Son by the grace of the Holy Spirit is expressed in the religious vows which, on the wavelength of Mary's "Yes", must also be lived as a people and for all peoples. *They must be lived now and "at the hour of our death".*

Mary's words "Let it be to me according to your word," in Greek: "katà to réma tu". The same expression recurs, again in Luke's gospel, in the episode of the presentation of Jesus in the Temple, where Simeon says:

> Lord, now lettest thou thy servant depart in peace according to thy word (Lk 2:29).

In the traditional translation – "Now lettest" – it would seem that Simeon is making a request. Actually the Greek verb is in the indicative mood, as in the above translation. Simeon is saying that the Lord has let him touch the summit of fullness. Indeed, his contemplation of the Child, of the glory of this Son for all the nations, for all peoples, is already an anticipation of the fullness of the Christian community after the resurrection.

Simeon anticipates, as it were, the fullness that Mary in her divine maternity brings by virtue of her "fiat". And he says: "Your Word, Lord, has filled me, and now I am with you forever. For me there is no longer either death or life; the entire past has been a preparation for this moment."

Death is the fulfilment of life. It is those "labour pains" in which the fullness of life is about to be manifested. In them our "Yes", joined to Mary's "Yes" at the foot of the cross, unites with Jesus' "Yes" to the Father: *"Father, into thy hands I commit my spirit"* (Lk 23:46).

Every day we die in some way to things, to vanity, to worldliness, to carnal desires, to sensuality. If we live as a spiritual sacrifice in keeping with Paul's invitation – "Do not be conformed to this world" (Rom 12:2) – we shall be dying every day and at the same pace growing into the fullness of true life.

May Mary, then, be near us on this journey whose culminating moment is death! We know that it is difficult to experience death this way; it is even humanly impossible, for in each one of us there resides the fear, horror and hatred of death and of all that precedes or anticipates it, such as sickness, failure, loneliness and physical handicaps.

So, in prayer we ask for the gift of a new vision

and a new heart with which to face "the hour of our death" beginning with Mary's "fiat" to Simeon's *"Nunc dimittis"* and finally to Jesus' words: "Father, into thy hands I commit my spirit" (Lk 23:46).

THE REALITY OF THE CROSS

The loss of Jesus in the Temple (Lk 2:41-52)

"We entreat you, Mary, to help us in reflecting on such a sorrowful and mysterious episode of your life. You have taught us that in order to understand the mystery of your presence near the cross, we must refract it into other mysteries of your life. And so we see something of your suffering anticipated in the days during which you search for Jesus in Jerusalem. As we endeavour to penetrate this mystery, we ask to be able to treasure your secret with love and humility. We do not want to pry into the labyrinth of your soul. Our only desire is to be enlightened by your journey in order to comprehend the words you have spoken; for having spoken them, you have consigned them to us that we may savour their meaning.

Grant us a share in the maternal love with which you live in obscurity and suffering together with your Son. Grant that there may be no element of indiscretion or excess in our search, but that it may be filled with praise, respect and reverence for the living mystery that you are and for the mystery that we, your children, are, who now enter upon your journey. Amen."

Before beginning our meditation on the Gospel text, I would like to explain to you the "Map of our Spiritual Journey" (see p. 10) which I have designed as a help in better understanding the unity of the things we are experiencing during these days. At the centre of the "map" there is the cross, and at the foot of the cross John and Mary. The rays surrounding signify the light that she radiates to the world and to humanity. The "map" is divided into two parts: on the right side, "the woman"; on the left, "among her people". This title is repeated in another form: on the right, "Mary's journey"; on the left, "with men and women of all times". The "map" is to be used as a root that begins below. There we find "the three groanings" that tend upwards. From them begins a winding course from left to right. On the left are the women of all times represented by women portrayed in the Gospels on which we have meditated. On the right is Mary's light in which each of the figures is reflected, either as light or in contrast to the light. The last line leads to Mary of Magdala, passing below the cross and through the cross to the resurrection.

In the middle, likewise from below upwards, some stages indicate our journey as suggested by various Gospel passages.

The Gospel message on the "map" which will now be ours for reflection is that of the loss of Jesus in the Temple, an account that challenges our exegetical ability and moves us intimately.

> Now his parents went to Jerusalem every year at the feast of the Passover. And when he was twelve old, they went up according to custom; and when the feast was ended, as they were returning, the boy Jesus stayed behind in Jerusalem. His parents did not know it, but supposing him to be in the company they went a day's journey, and they sought him among their kinsfolk and acquaintances; and when they did not find him, they returned to Jerusalem, seeking him. After

three days they found him in the temple, sitting among the teachers, listening to them and asking them questions; and all who heard him were amazed at his understanding and his answers. And when they saw him they were astonished; and his mother said to him, "Son, why have you treated us so? Behold, your father and I have been looking for you anxiously." And he said to them, "How is it that you sought me? Did you not know that I must be in my Father's house?" And they did not understand the saying which he spoke to them. And he went down with them and came to Nazareth, and was obedient to them; and his mother kept all these things in her heart.

And Jesus increased in wisdom and in stature, and in favour with God and man (Lk 2:41-52).

The text

I suggest that we do a reading of the text, taking some words one after the other and asking ourselves what they are saying to us.

We also have to keep in mind some conclusions of exegetical research. Scholars like Laurentin and Feuillet who have spent much time on this page of the Gospel agree in saying that it has a Johannine flavour: it contains concepts and words which resemble those of the Fourth Gospel in aspect, resonance and depth.

In addition, scholars affirm that this passage hints at the principal Christological mysteries: divine paternity and sonship and Jesus' death and resurrection. It is an anticipated meditation on the passion and the mystery of Christ. At the same time it shows how difficult it is for the human being to comprehend the mystery of God in his own history.

With her "Yes" Mary had already accepted the mystery of God incarnate in history at least in its *global proclamation*. Nevertheless, in this episode Mary experiences in common with all human beings how hard it is to accept the fact that the mystery of God, welcomed in general, turns out differently than we would have expected. We too find it difficult to accept the fact that the Church is as the is, that Jesus Christ has manifested himself as he did and not differently, that the mystery of our life is not as we would have it!

This passage leads us, therefore, to the threshold of the personal secret of Mary, which we would be afraid to penetrate if she herself in her goodness did not encouragingly place her hand on our head, pardoning any improper words we may say and helping our heart to express itself.

Jerusalem and the Passover

"*Now his parents went to Jerusalem every year.*" To the Hebrew, Jerusalem is a magical word. Even today it is the symbol of a whole reality, of an existence, of a history and of a hope. To underline the importance of the theme, the evangelist repeats the name of *Jerusalem* three times: "Now his parents went to *Jerusalem*... the boy Jesus stayed behind in *Jerusalem*... they returned to Jerusalem seeking him."

This word claims our reflection not solely because of its significance as the central location in salvation history but also as one of the poles of the infancy narratives and then of Jesus' life.

Jesus' infancy begins in Jerusalem in the Temple with the apparition of the angel to Zechariah. It moves to Judaea, to Zechariah's house, then to Mary's house in Nazareth and again to Judaea when Mary visits her cousin Elizabeth, then to Bethlehem for the birth of Jesus and back to Jerusalem for the presentation in the Temple. It returns to Nazareth and later transfers to Jerusalem where it concludes with the episode on which we are meditating.

In summary: *the story of Jesus' infancy begins in Jerusalem, reaches its climax in Jerusalem at the presentation in the Temple and ends in Jerusalem.*

According to Luke's account (chapter 24), *Jesus' earthly life will terminate in Jerusalem.*

In Jerusalem will begin the history of the Church (Acts 1) which will be extended to the ends of the earth.

The "holy city" is, then, the place where God's designs are revealed, the place in which God's plan is initiated, reaches its culmination and unfolds. Consequently it remains the icon of the manifestation of divine glory in history. In our episode, therefore, Jesus reveals something of his mystery.

"For the feast of the Passover": These too are words very rich in meaning. The feast of the Passover is the great principal feast of the Hebrews (this is Luke's first mention of the Passover and foreshadows Jesus' last Passover). We can say that Jesus' life is framed between this Passover experienced in childhood and the final one before his death. For the primitive Church, which listened to and repeated the account of the evangelist, to know that Jesus was in Jerusalem for the feast of the Passover was equivalent to understanding all the potential of the paschal mystery that was about to become manifest.

The feast forms the backdrop of this episode,

and Jesus certainly celebrated it with deep and intense emotion, mysteriously foreseeing that it presaged his own "passages" to the Father, a passage that would recall and bring to fulfillment the signs inherent in this Passover of his boyhood.

"When the feast was ended... the boy Jesus stayed behind in Jerusalem. His parents did not know it." The verb "stayed" in Greek is *upémeine* which means to "persevere", to continue at an action that can be difficult yet important. From it is derived the noun "patience", *upomoné*; the root of the verb is "dwell", *méno*. The subtle, philological connection with John's Gospel makes us reflect. "Dwell" is a typical Johannine word, expressing the Father's dwelling in the Son, as well as man's dwelling in the Son and in the Word. Jesus' remaining in the Temple implies a kind of dwelling; he makes Jerusalem his dwelling because it is his place, it has something to do with him, it is his natural habitat (and, in fact, he will afterwards say why).

Here the mysterious association of affinity and residence between Jesus and the Temple is indicated. Jesus' irresistible attraction to the Temple stands in contrast to the incomprehension of his parents: "His parents did not know it;" in Greek: *uk égnossan*, they did not know it, they were not aware of it.

We are before a great mystery. What happened to Mary is no trifling matter. Normally mothers know what kind of things are attractive to their children and have an idea of where they could have gone once they have slipped supervision and escaped. While it is true that, especially in the oriental world, a twelve-year old possessed a certain independence, still it seems that this was the first time he had been to Jerusalem and the parents would have had to be attentive.

It could be said – and if I find it rather hard to say – that Joseph and Mary had lost the view of the whole, the thrust of the situation; they had missed the essential. Is it possible, we ask ourselves, that they had not understood the power of attraction that the Temple exercised over Jesus? Is it possible that they did not recognize the irresistible fascination that would rivet him, as it were, to the Temple?

In search of God

"Supposing him to be in the company they went a day's journey, and they sought him among their kinsfolk and acquaintances." The verb "supposing" seems to reinforce the idea that the parents did not at all think of the possibility of Jesus' remaining in Jerusalem. In translation the text gives the impression that Joseph and Mary had spent a carefree day without becoming concerned about his whereabouts. The Greek text, however, presents the fact a bit differently. The parents see that he is not there; they ask themselves where he might be, but it is clear that in the meantime the caravan must continue its journey. They look for him, therefore, while the caravan is moving on, and by the time they have verified the boy's absence it is already evening.

On the other hand, it seems strange to us that Joseph and Mary would have sought solutions that are not plausible to us, for we cannot bring ourselves to imagine that Jesus could have gone his way chattering right and left! What does the attitude of the parents tells us? All of us have experienced losing the point of a situation without it being our fault, simply because it did not dawn on us. We do not always succeed in evaluating events in their entirety, and the moment arises when we strike our breast because we have missed something which logically we ought not to have overlooked. We had much to do that day and were not attentive to a certain person, whereas it would have been normal to give him our attention, and so on.

Mary shares in our fragility because she herself has passed through this moment of losing the wider sense of the situation. Perhaps a little reflection on her part would have sufficed: "Jesus stood almost motionless in the Temple; we could not move him from the spot; he surely stayed there!"

If our Lady has experienced such a harsh moment of distress, humiliation and sorrow, we too can be excused; we too must realize that despite all efforts our poor nature will often not succeed in grasping the real core of the situation. Mary takes us by the hand and teaches us humility: the humility and humiliation that can come to us from people who criticize our blunder, our deficient power of intuition, our forgetfulness, our lack of attention to a certain person in an important circumstance.

Perhaps the people in the caravan criticized Mary: "Look, it happened even to her. Things cannot always be in her favour...," and so forth. Here Mary is truly *among* her people: living, sharing, suffering, being criticized, feeling bewildered, blaming herself somehow. – How did I ever do that? How was it possible?

"They sought him among their kinsfolk and acquaintances; and when they did not find him, they returned to Jerusalem, seeking him." "Seeking him" is a verb in the imperfect tense in Greek: *anazétun.* It denotes a continuous search, without

stop. *"Seeking him"*: I take this phrase up again and place it in relation to Jesus' reply: *"How is it that you sought me?"* The search for Jesus is the search for God and involves a person's entire life journey. We recall that his verb is the same one Jesus uses in his first question put to the two disciples who approached him: "What do you seek?" (Jn 1:37).

Searching is a symbol of man's journey toward truth, and the search of Mary and Joseph is marked by affection, love and anxiety. In a word, it is characterized by all the valour, beauty and echoes of a quest.

For this reason, Jesus' reproach – *"How is it that you sought me?"* – is very strange and disconcerts us. In order to understand it we probably should consider the various meaning of this verb in John's Gospel and the diverse ways of seeking Jesus, especially after his resurrection when Mary Magdalene, for example, seeks the living Jesus among the dead.

There is a wrong way of seeking Jesus. Such a search invites reprimand because it amount to claiming that God should act according to our ideas rather than according to his designs. Here we are given an intimation of the real mystery of a search, which is essentially the fundamental human striving toward what is true. It can, however, turn into a void if the true is sought where it cannot be found or in things in which it cannot manifest itself.

Mary, who had to discern the meaning of her search, can enlighten us in so many of the frenzied searchings for Jesus that we undertake. For example, when we endeavour to find grace, consolation, clarity about our life, assurance that we are on the right path, solutions to our problems, when we already have all these things, or can discover them plainly and easily in an authoritative decision or in some already manifest reality. But not wanting to accept this, we continue our search under the alleged excuse that we need more light from the Lord.

In other words, we have difficulty in accepting God's workings in our own life because it is easier to assent to him in his divine totality and abstractness that in an actual history that is different from what we would like. Obedience to God is acceptance of his self-revelation in the reality of *this Jesus* crucified and humbled, of *this* poor, weak Church, of *this* ailment-ridden body of mind, of *this* laborious spiritual life of mine. We would always prefer to encounter God elsewhere and this causes us to lose sight of the point of the actual situation. Only when we admit to ourselves the fact that our search is anxious concern and not a true search for we become aware that substantially we already have what we were seeking.

"After three days they found him." Again it is stressed that Mary and Joseph did not know where to seek. Maybe they went to the families who had given them hospitality. In any case, they could not immediately account for the fact. Hence their state of not knowing mentioned earlier – *His parents did know it* – continues, as it were.

Jesus permitted his parents to experience the dark cloud, the distressing dryness and the mounting pain of those who seek the Lord without finding him. Jesus is, therefore, near anyone who endures this suffering and experiences God's mysterious silence. For three days Mary and Joseph no longer heard his voice to which they were accustomed from morning till night: the voice, the Word is silent. It is silent while they conjure up the most dismal and upsetting conjectures; their anxiety is extremely painful; it is a most acute trial of faith.

Surely we would have entertained thoughts that did not at all occur to Mary: "God has abandoned me. He did not give me the mission I was expecting. Perhaps I did not know the right response. Now my life is a failure!" Then our thinking becomes muddled and we are seized with fear. All this prompts us to contemplate Mary's humble silence, a silence that does not ask "Why?" any more than she will ask that question at the foot of the cross. In prayer, and only there, we can sense the mystery of Mary's silence. Mary does not question herself at all, nor brood, nor stop to think of the blunders she may possibly have committed. Had she done so, it would not have added a bit to the efficacy of her search, any more than all our thinking can add a bit of weight to our actions. At the most it can rob us of more than a bit of our sleep.

Here we see that Mary is very different from us but at the same time encouraging. She seems to be saying to us: "Do what you are doing – *age quod agis*. If you have to write, write. If the telephone rings, answer it. Receive the people who call on you. Do not build castles in the air, for that is useless." Mary, I believe, gives us the priceless hint to remain at our present task without pausing over the past or indulging in evasive plans for the future. It is the most genuine way of living through and embracing God's silence.

In addition to their psychological significance, into which we have tried to delve, the words "after three days" also have a theological value which was obvious to the early Christian community. They are the three days of Jesus' passion and death. The Church has gone through this anguish of the passion and death; the Apostles have also experienced it. The Church continues to relive it in dark and obscure times. We too live it in our life united to Good Friday, to Jesus' passion which is foreshadowed here: "Days are coming in which the sun will be darkened, the Son of man's voice will be silent and deep darkness will envelop the earth." The Good Friday of history repeats itself, also for us , for our community, for our Church. It is useless to ask why, although the moment of clarification may arrive. There are times in which we have to keep on humbly holding the plough in our hands and making the furrow, inch by inch, because we are not in a position to do otherwise.

They found him in the Temple. This is the decisive word at the heart of this entire episode. In a certain sense it was implied, for in speaking of Jesus and the feast it was impossible not to think of the Temple. It emerges now, however, to emphasize precisely that God permits trial and moments of diminished light.

The Temple is understood as a place and manifestation of the Father's presence, sign of the sovereignty of God, the only Lord, of God who alone is God and may only be God.

The Temple is a sign of the Absolute who governs all history, who divides humanity and human hearts into those who accept this Absolute and believe, and those who do not accept and condemn themselves.

The mystery of Jesus

He was sitting among the teachers, listening to them and asking them questions; and all who heard him were amazed at his understanding and his answers. It has always struck me as strange that we are first told that Jesus was "listening to them, and asking them questions" and then that they "were astonished at his... replies".

What is the message of this scene? Jesus is the wisdom that astounds man. It is the same wonder at the divine that we feel before the miracles and all the great manifestations of God. Here Jesus manifests himself in the temple, anticipating the manifestation of his wisdom in the temple spoken of by John in chapters 7 and 8 of his Gospel. His wisdom is not that of one who has studied: "How is it that this man has learning, when he has never studied?" (Jn 7:15). Rather, it comes from the Father: "My teaching is not mine, but his who sent me" (Jn 7:16).

Here Jesus reveals his wisdom in anticipation of his public life and his teaching; his is the word that comes from above and astonishes by its newness.

We ask ourselves what these questions and this intelligence must have been. As we know, the rabbis proceeded in a casuist manner, I think that Jesus' questions must have been similar to some of the ones he would pose later in his life and were distinguished by simplicity, clarity and the power to penetrate the obvious. Jesus possessed synesis, the ability to see through to the profound meaning of things.

It is interesting that he begins by listening. He starts out very modestly and then interrogates when he detects the weak spot in the traditional, stale answer. This is the secret that will make his future preaching so fascinating.

In our present religious, spiritual and theological education we are threatened by the danger of having too many books and doing less and less thinking! Every new book is based on another one or on two or three others. Sometimes I wonder if even be bishops write too many documents, which then have to be taken into account. It is not difficult to say something new, but it does prove difficult to have to keep up on all the previously published documents!

Since Vatican Council II up to the present there has been such an avalanche of publications that we are in serious danger of being suffocated. This hinders personal meditation and deep reflection on God's Word. Often priests justly complain to me that they do not know how to find time to read the encyclicals, apostolic exhortations, pastoral letters, documents, commentaries, and so forth. Generally I advise them to limit themselves to whatever best serves their spiritual growth or ministry. We ought to free ourselves from slavery to books and instead look at Jesus crucified. Contemplating him inwardly should evoke our own spiritual understanding, which will be strengthened by all that can truly help and stimulate.

By this I do not intend to discourage those who produce teaching aids or urge bishops to stop writing pastoral letters. I do, however, want to recall that Jesus had a mind that listened and asked questions based first of all on his knowledge of the Father. That is the main thing. Even if we do not succeed in citing all the books that deal with a certain them, the Lord will undoubtedly give us the light we need to discover the depths of meaning of what we ought to say.

And when they saw him they were astonished; and his mother said to him, "Son, why have you treated us so? Behold, your father and I have been looking for you anxiously."

This is not to reprimand, but the words are severe enough, as though to mean: we do not understand. The expression "how worried" is very painful. In Greek it is *odunómenoi*, a word which we find again in Luke (16:24) in the account of the rich man who cries out, "I am *in anguish* in these flames." It indicates a state of excruciating inner suffering. The same word is used in the *Acts of the Apostles* when Paul announces to the elders of Ephesus that he is about to depart for Jerusalem and they will never see him again. Here he was hinting at his death: "They all wept... because of the word he had spoken, that they should see his face no more" (20:37-38).

But Jesus' reply does not correspond to the excitability of the question, and this is a great mystery. Jesus could have answered: "Yes, I understand. I am sorry, but I had to do it. You could have guessed it."

Instead he uses strong language: *How is it that you sought me? Did you not know that I must be in my Father's house?* According to Feuillet, a Biblical scholar of great merit:

> Finding himself in the Temple in Jerusalem, symbol of the heavenly Father's house and, therefore, symbol of the true dwelling-place of the Son of God, Jesus explains to the bewildered Mary and Joseph: 'Do you not know that I need to remain with my Father in his house?' There is no doubt: ... this passage was understood in this sense by all the Greek Fathers without exception, from Origen to St John Damascene, and by all the Latin Fathers up to the 12th century... And these mysterious words of Jesus have a two-fold meaning. The

more obvious is, as Lagrange says: 'Jesus smilingly answers that it was only to be expected that he would be found near his Father.' But one intuitively senses a more profound meaning, a veiled allusion to that return of Jesus to his Father's house which is so often mentioned in John's Gospel. And this formula – 'I need to, I must, it is necessary' for me to be occupied with my Father's affairs – is the key formula of the two-fold mystery of the passion and resurrection by which Jesus will return to the Father."

(A. Feuillet, *Jésus et sa Mère*,
Ed. Gabalda, Paris 1974, pp. 73-74.)

This statement is, therefore, indicative *above all of the ontological mystery of Jesus* (I am with the Father, I am in the Father, I must be in the Father's house). Until how he had not said this, and even if it had been said in the angel's announcement to Mary, it would have been without effect. Here, however, he makes it know with extreme force. We would have preferred Jesus to prepare his parents for what would happen in Jerusalm, becuase it is always difficult for us to accept the manner in which Jesus, who is free-willed and free person, deals with us.

In the second place Jesus' reply foreshadows the mystery of *redemption*: it must be, it is necessary. This is the expression that we shall find again at the end of Luke's Gospel referring to the paschal mystery: "Was it not necessary that the Christ should suffere these things and enter his glory?" (Lk 24:26).

But they did not understand the saying. Faced with such a blunt manifestatioin of the mystery and its consequences, Mary and Joseph do not understand. They still have a way to go. The frankness with which the Gospel is expressed here almost makes us speechless.

They did not understand are the words Luke uses for the incomprehension of the Apostles when Jesus explains to them that the Son of man must suffer: "But they did not understand this saying" (9:45); "They understand none of these things" (18:34).

It shows how we grope when faced with the mystery of Jesus' death and resurrection. Mary and Joseph, though submissive, humble and receptive, have experienced before us this shudder at failing to understand.

"Mary, so often we do not understand. Grant that the humility and suffering or your not understanding may be our support when we are impatient, proud and at times arrogant because we do not understand. With your gentleness and perseverance, with your patient silence, heal the rebellion that often accompanies our reflections on our life, the life of our communities and of the Church. Let us share in your "Yes" which remains such in the most painful darkness and incomprehension suffered, even to the cross and resurrection."

TOWARD THE RESURRECTION

Mary of Magdala (Jn 20:11-18)

Through the intercession of Mary of Magdala we ask to enter into Mary's sorrow and joy, to enter this sorrow and this joy as they are expressed in the body and history of the Church:

"Pray for us now, O Mary, Mother of God. Grant us a share in your suffering and in your praise, in your sorrow and in your exultation. Keep alive in our hearts, even after these days, the mystery of your presence near the cross."

In our meditations we have constantly kept in mind the scene of Mary at the foot of the cross without, however, dealing directly with it. Actually, I prefer to leave it to each one of you to contemplate this mystery so filled with love and pain. Instead we shall meditate together on a final gospel passage, that of the appearance of the Risen Lord to Mary of Magdala:

But Mary stood weeping outside the tomb, and as she wept she stooped to look into the tomb; and she saw two angels in white, sitting where the body of Jesus had lain, one at the head, the other at the feet. They said to her, "Woman, why are you weeping?" "They have taken my Lord away," she replied, "and I don't know where they have put him." Saying this, she turned round and saw Jesus standing there, though she did not realise that it was Jesus. Jesus said to her, "Woman, why are you weeping? Who are you looking for?" Supposing him to be the gardener, she said, "Sir, if you have taken him away, tell me where you have put him, and I will go and remove him." Jesus said, "Mary!" She turned round then and said to him in Hebrew, "Rab-bóni!" – which means Master. Jesus said to her, "Do not hold me, for I have not yet ascended to the Father; but go to my brethren, and say to them, I am ascending to my Father and your Father, to my God and your God." Mary Magdalene went and said to the disciples, "I have seen the Lord," and she told them that he had said these things to her (Jn 20:11-18).

Mary seeks Jesus

This passage, very rich in allusions and symbols, begins with, "But Mary," that is, in contrast to Simon Peter and John who have seen the empty tomb, have understood, have tried to draw conclusions about it and then have gone home. Not Mary. That is characteristic of this woman who is simply called Mary. At the beginning of the chapter her name was mentioned in full: Mary of Magdala. Now that she is only called Mary, we can glimpse behind her other feminine personalities and in her we discover some aspects that conjure up Mary of Bethany and even Mary of Nazareth.

She *"stood outside"*. This verb in the imperfect is striking and makes us visualize her as immobile, as though planted there unable to move. Evidently she has been overcome by a strong seizure of emotion that holds her fast. Peter and John have entered the tomb, but she remains somewhat outside the mystery. This too has its significance.

"Weeping outside the tomb." Mary's weeping is mentioned four times in this text: She "stood weeping outside;" "as she wept," "Woman, why are

you weeping," ask the angels, and Jesus repeats this same question. The evangelist notes this four times because he wants to make us reflect. We can take this occasion to recall other weeping persons recorded in the gospels. The weeping of the widow of Nain, for example, or Mary's weeping at the tomb of her brother Lazarus, which arouses Jesus' feelings. In this episode Jesus managed to control his own emotions until he saw Mary weeping. Then he was shaken and broke out in tears.

Weeping is a mysterious manner of communicating and it hits us when we no longer succeed in holding the logical and emotional thread of things together. Just to see a person weeping communicates a great deal to those who witness it. There is even a true and proper *art* of weeping that at the right moment can stir up the emotions of a group.

Weeping does not say anything and at the same time it says a lot. When we happen to be with someone who suddenly weeps, either we become involved in the same emotion and begin to weep with the person, or if we are on a different wavelength we feel embarrassment. In either case, weeping does not leave us indifferent.

Recall also Jesus weeping outside Jerusalem. In a certain sense this is the most mysterious incident in Jesus' life. Jesus weeps although nothing has happened. He weeps from the vehement emotion provoked in him by the difference between what he sees – to all appearances, peace, serenity, quiet living – and what will happen. It is a weeping caused by profound penetration into the dramatic meaning of things and of life.

Amplifying our discourse, we can note the element of weeping reappearing in many religious events (many of which are probably fabricated). Think of the weeping of the Madonna, of the tears shed during the centuries and even in our times by some statues. All this shows us the creative and evocative power of weeping.

Why does Mary of Magdala weep? On the one hand she herself explains it to the angels: "They have taken my Lord away, and I don't know where they have put him." Her tears, then, spring from what we have called the sense of belonging, the profound awareness of being related to someone who at a certain moment is no longer there. This woman had grown through an intense experience of conversion. For the first time in her life she had found someone who understood her to the depths, who had had confidence in her, who had given her a sense of identity and restored her dignity. All this gave birth in her to the sense of belonging to Christ, a relationship by which she felt defined.

Now she thinks that this experience will be lacking to her and she feels herself collapsing. It is the downfall of the foundation upon which she had constructed her personal dignity and likewise the collapse of the sincere, disinterested love that she had experienced from Jesus.

Consequently, her violent emotional reaction is understandable. Note that here she is the only one weeping. We are not told that Peter and John wept, perhaps because at this point their experience was not of comparable intensity. But it is recorded that Peter wept on the day of the passion, for it was the moment in which he discovered the gulf between the love of his Lord and his own unworthiness.

The weeping of Mary of Magdala, like that of Peter during the passion, arises from a discovery of truth. It is a salutary weeping, expressing what could never be expressed in words. Not without reason, the great saints have experienced this weeping as a grace, and mystics speak of a weeping that is a "gift" – the gift of tears.

St Charles is frequently portrayed weeping before the crucifix. In his spiritual diary St Ignatius of Loyola notes almost daily: tears, tears, tears during Mass, tears during thanksgiving. These are gifts of intense religious emotion on perceiving truth and the disturbing links between the various aspects of truth. Basically the weeping of Mary of Magdala here is somewhat like the wine of Cana; it is that necessary "extra" which manifests full emotional involvement.

"Teach us, Mary of Magdala, to enter with this total involvement of ourselves into the mystery of Jesus, my Lord, my Saviour, my Justice, my Truth, my Love, my Spouse, my Redemption, my Salvation, my Light, my Repose, my Peace." St Ambrose, who often speaks in his works of his own weeping and that of the Church, liked to address Christ in similar words.

"She stooped to look into the tomb, and saw two angels." Every detail is attentively noticed. At first Mary stood outside, then she stooped and finally she saw. What does this gesture mean? Each one of us must admit that these almost minute details, whose significance John became aware of in contemplation, penetrate us only by means of lengthy periods of prayer.

This woman stoops before the tomb. She has the courage to look still more deeply into the mystery of the death that frightens her. As far as we can gather from the account, Peter and John were not afraid to enter and look. She, however, was not up to it and only now dares it. For her it is truly a surrendering of her being to the mystery that she had rejected with all her might and did not want to admit – the death of her Lord. Now on the contrary, this mystery begins to light up her life, to illuminate and reclothe it with light. Her stooping is a ford of faith. Had she remained turned in on herself, her weeping would gradually have turned into rage, anger and vexation against herself and others. Instead, her courageous act of bending toward the darkness of the sepulchre begins to reveal to her that the darkness contains light, companionship and life.

Who are the two angels? A woman author of a lengthy commentary on John's gospel recognizes in them the angels who accompanied Jesus during his earthly life. Now they show themselves to the woman because she has had the courage to look into the mystery of her Lord's death. However that may be, the angels are a first proclamation that the negative interpretation of suffering is wrong, that there is a positive aperture, a gleam of light.

"Why are you weeping?" "They have taken my Lord away," she replied, *"and I don't know where they have laid him."* The dialogue is brief and does not seem to reassure the woman. At any rate, the fact is that she does not wait for a response. She is still troubled by various thoughts. Light is dawning on her only gradually.

Jesus reveals himself to Mary

"Saying this, she turned round and saw Jesus standing, but she did not know that it was Jesus." She loved him intensely and sought him, but her anxiety to settle her case and her desire to find

Jesus prevents her from seeing and understanding that Jesus is already there.

Herein lies a basic detail that has its parallel, it seems to me, in the episode of the disciples of Emmaus. Only when the mind has calmed down and the context can be clarified, when the person has abandoned the rigidity that deems salvation possible only in one particular way, only then does he become aware that salvation is already present.

Deep down, there is some humour in the description of this woman who wants Jesus with all her strength and is disposed to do anything whatever to have at least his corpse, but when he is standing right before her she does not recognize him! The first glimmers and the first rays are not effective; she insists on her own kind of search. And Jesus, what does he do? He repeats the angels' question: "Woman, why are you weeping? Whom do you seek?" Like the angels, he asks the general reason for her weeping; then he proceeds to make the personal motive emerge: *"Whom do you seek?"*

It is interesting to compare Jesus' question here toward the end of the gospel with the one he asked the two disciples at the beginning of the gospel: *"What* do you want?" The difference is that in the early stages of the journey Jesus asked, "What do you want?" whereas here at the very end of the way he asks, "Whom do you seek?" Jesus accentuates that salvation is a Person, the very Person standing before the woman.

Jesus said, "Mary!" We could have imagined other ways of presenting himself: "Why are you so slow in believing? I am risen," or the like.

Jesus chooses the most personal and most direct way – calling a person by name. In itself this does not say a thing, because anyone can pronounce

"Mary". This does not explain the resurrection nor the fact that it is the Lord addressing her. Nevertheless we all understand, without anyone's having to expound it for us, that this address by name at this moment, in this situation, with that voice, in that tone is the most personal manner of revelation and concerns not simply Jesus but *Jesus in his relationship to her.*

He manifests himself as her Lord, the one she is looking for. This personalising of the relationship between them is truly marvellous and is a very bold image of the entire life of grace. The life of grace is the Lord calling us by name in our hearts with the same love as the One crucified and risen, that is, with the whole weight of the redemption.

"Lord, let me not be deaf to this name that you pronounce within me! Make me listen to it with all the fascination and evocative power with which it is so full!"

Mary too immediately reacts in a most personal manner: "Rabboni!" meaning *my Master.* In an instant is said everything she could possibly say about herself, her love, her dedication.

"Do not hold me." Jesus helps her to rise still higher, for although Mary has made immense progress she has not yet grasped the profound meaning of what has taken place.

In our life too it often happens that we think we have comprehended everything whereas we still have a long way to go. Mary of Magdala has yet to learn that Christ is related to the Father and that only when he has fully returned to the Father will his work be definitively completed.

In praise of God the Father

"Go to my brethren." Now Mary has understood and will, therefore, be the first to announce to the disciples God's universal plan, his divine Fatherhood and the brotherhood of all human beings in Christ, which derives from the fulfillment of this plan.

This truth in all its implications could even seem to be too much at one time. Jesus knows, however, that Mary of Magdala – and every woman who goes this way – is able to bear all the riches of this mystery, even though she will not know how to explain it fully in all its exegetical implications. She can be a bearer of the mystery and proclaimer of Christ's resurrection.

You are women of the resurrection, you who have had this encounter with Christ, an encounter from which you have received the message of joy and hope as well as the certainty that God's plan will be fulfilled and is already being infallibly fulfilled.

Each of you ought to be a witness to the truth that the plan of history opens out onto the fullness of God; a witness to this message whose focus is the Father: "I am ascending to my Father and your Father, to my God and your God." So our meditations conclude with the word "Father".

We have said much about Mary of Nazareth, about the woman and her children, about humanity. We have spoken about Christ. All this is related to the mystery of the Father from whom everything descends and to whom it all returns. Praise addressed to the Father is the final, decisive word, a word that sums up the whole of salvation history, for it gathers together in a hymn, sung by saved humanity the gratitude of all, with Mary, in the power and grace of the Holy Spirit, through Christ.

"To God, the Father of mercies, light and source of all good, Lord of history and of the universe, goal of the entire human journey, we lift our praise. To you, Father, be praise in the Church and in the world, in earthly history and in heaven. May Mary, Mother of Jesus, praise you; may the angels praise you; may the thrones and dominions praise you; may the saints praise you; may our deceased praise you; may everyone we meet praise you, that we all may be able to unite in a hymn acknowledging the fullness of glory which your Son communicates to us in the grace of the Spirit who animates our hearts. Amen."